# Latina Teachers in the Deep South

# Critical Studies of Latinxs in the Americas

Yolanda Medina and Margarita Machado-Casas
Series Editors
Vol. 32

Vanessa E. Vega

# Latina Teachers in the Deep South

## Testimonios, Cuentos y Consejos

**PETER LANG**

Lausanne - Berlin - Bruxelles - Chennai - New York - Oxford

Library of Congress Cataloging-in-Publication Data

Names: Vega, Vanessa E., author.
Title: Latina teachers in the Deep South : testimonios, cuentos y consejos
/ Vanessa E. Vega.
Description: First edition. | New York : Peter Lang, [2024] | Series:
Critical Studies of Latinxs in the Americas, 2372-6822 ; volume 32 |
Includes bibliographical references.
Identifiers: LCCN 2023052099 (print) | LCCN 2023052100 (ebook) | ISBN
9781433193156 (paperback : alk. paper) | ISBN 9781433193149 (hardback :
alk. paper) | ISBN 9781433193118 (pdf) | ISBN 9781433193125 (epub)
Subjects: LCSH: Feminist anthropology–Southern States. | Hispanic American
teachers–Ethnic identity–Southern States. | Minority women
teachers–Southern States–Social conditions. | Young adult literature,
American–Study and teaching. | American literature–Hispanic American
women authors–History and criticism. | Marginality, Social, in
literature. | Love, Maternal, in literature. | Belonging (Social
psychology) in literature. | Power (Social sciences) in literature. |
Narrative inquiry (Research method)
Classification: LCC GN33.8 .V44 2024 (print) | LCC GN33.8 (ebook) | DDC
371.10092/520975–dc23/eng/20240108
LC record available at https://lccn.loc.gov/2023052099
LC ebook record available at https://lccn.loc.gov/2023052100

DOI 10.3726/b21457


Bibliographic information published by the Deutsche Nationalbibliothek.
The German National Library lists this publication in the German
National Bibliography; detailed bibliographic data is available
on the Internet at http://dnb.d-nb.de.

Cover design by Peter Lang Group AG


ISSN 2372-6822 (print) ISSN 2372-6830 (online)
ISBN 9781433193156 (paperback)
ISBN 9781433193149 (hardback)
ISBN 9781433193118 (ebook)
ISBN 9781433193125 (epub)
DOI 10.3726/b21457

© 2024 Peter Lang Group AG, Lausanne
Published by Peter Lang Publishing Inc., New York, USA
info@peterlang.com – www.peterlang.com

# CONTENTS

# DEDICATION

This book is dedicated to my family, near and far: to Viviana, luz y aire de mi vida, for her endless patience and encouragement; to Mami y Papi, for their endless love and trust; to Benji, Susan, and the Vega clan, for their faith in me; and to my familia's mujeres resistentes (Aby, Abuela Petra, Abuela Carmen, Titi Marta, Edimar, Rosadel, Mama Blanca, Titi Myrna, Blanquita, Dr. Nydia Cummings, Titi Maggie, Ileanita), for guiding me with ancestral love and light . . . this is for us.

# INTRODUCTION

When I first moved to Birmingham, Alabama in 2007, I was intrigued by the notion of living in an area rich in racial courage and history. I envisioned a progressive space rife with thriving Black pride – I would be remiss if I didn't shamelessly admit expecting to see a contemporary version of Angela Davis; not necessarily physical evidence of lustrous coils framing the contours of an afro, but certainly the type of fierce convictions that make a body walk taller and more confidently. I imagined White individuals working in tandem within the knowledge that civil rights had been fought and won inside the stories their parents and grandparents told. The stories of Black teachers would be tinged with pain yet brimming with power and hope. I anticipated living in an area where there might be a burgeoning Latinx community. I realized that no place would ever be like Miami, Florida, where I had begun my teaching career with the explicit intention of teaching Latinx kids.

I distinctly recall daydreaming about wearing combat boots; I would be, after all, working at a university where liberal minds and attire would likely prevail. Like the civil rights warriors before me, I too would celebrate my rebelliousness by sassing my unique Puerto Rican style among the hallways of the School of Education. I never imagined that my first year would be tinged with racial microaggressions. There is likely still a letter that resides in my personnel file detailing how my attire was offensive to a school administrator. Never mind that the administrator who complained was a mature Black man in the very system whose students marched the streets for civil rights so many years before. Never mind that the offense purportedly detailed the tightness of my pants, which my thick Latina thighs have always struggled to contain. Never mind that my White female boss likely influenced the genesis of that letter. That letter resulted in multiple self-reflections, including how my body was policed and what it meant to be an outsider even when my White Puerto Rican skin was supposed to mask my Latinidad. I was used to blending among other Latinas that looked like and unlike me; I had experienced the isolation that came from the anglicization of my Spanglish language – but this was different, I was an adult now who wasn't supposed to crumble in defeat. I had to find another mask to protect myself from myself and others. I also had to cultivate allies, both Black and White.

I have always been deeply interested in the stories that cradle our individual experiences. Stories have always bridged my understanding of people, both similar and different than myself. They have, for example, allowed me to celebrate the complex differences that comprise the lives of narrators and characters residing in books. As a former English teacher and avid reader, it wasn't until I was in college that I recall reading *The House on Mango Street* (Cisneros, 1984) with a Latina protagonist, Esperanza, who validated the importance of my family. I saw myself in Esperanza, even though she was Mexican and not Puerto Rican like me. Much like Esperanza, I yearned for a place to call home. After nearly 15 years living in Alabama, I finally felt sufficiently comfortable to sprinkle Spanish phrases and words into conversations with some colleagues. I had forgotten what it felt like to peel the outer White mold of myself and let the Puerto Rican-ness shine through. This comfort eased my sense of being an outsider, which made me wonder what other Latina teachers felt like in settings where they were the minority. I wondered whether, like me, they felt isolated; if they had their Spanish shamed out of them; if they sacrificed their bilingual and bicultural identities to make room for an assimilated version of themselves. I wondered who their allies were and what narratives and counter-narratives they shared with or kept silenced from their family and friends. I also wondered how young adult fiction written by Latinas could provide a platform to explore their personal and schooling experiences; and how such critical exploration and dialogue among other Latina teachers could contribute to group solidarity.

# What About the Latina Teachers?

In the United States, students of Color comprise 51 % of students enrolled in public schools, however, teachers that are racial minorities make up only 20 % of teachers in public schools, 9 % of whom are Latinx (De Brey et al., 2019). Thus, while the student population continues to become more diverse, with Latinx students composing 26 % of students of Color enrolled in public schools in 2015 (De Brey et al., 2019, p. 52), teachers remain overwhelmingly White. According to Ingersoll, May, and Collins (2019), "minority teachers [including Latinx teachers] have significantly higher turnover than White teachers" (p. 1) that is primarily due to job dissatisfaction related to working, organizational, and school administration conditions (e.g., the ability for teachers to make decisions at their school). In addition, racial minority teachers leave the field of teaching at a rate that is 24 % greater than White teachers (Easton-Brooks, 2013; Kohli, 2018; Robinson, Paccione, & Rodriguez, 2003).

Interestingly, the Latinx population continues to grow in southern counties, to include those within states like Alabama where Latinx population growth ranked number five in the United States from 2000 to 2014 (UnidosUS, 2016; Stepler & Lopez, 2016). In 2011, Alabama attempted to fully enact stringent anti-immigration legislation (i.e., the Beason-Hammon Taxpayer and Citizen Protection Act, otherwise known as HB 56), which was mostly blocked, however, several provisions still remain in place (Sheets, 2017). Among other aspects, this legislation, originally dubbed the toughest anti-immigrant legislation in the U.S., required schools to identify students' documented status, prohibited individuals from providing transportation to undocumented people, and disallowed employers from hiring suspected undocumented people except for house-workers (e.g., housekeepers and lawn maintenance workers) (SPLC, 2021). The ramifications were immediate, with parents keeping their children home from school, local health clinics denying healthcare, and an increase of vigilantism and racial attacks toward the Latinx community (SPLC, 2021). The implicit outcome was for undocumented workers to self-deport and leave Alabama. The notable remnants of the legislation are that employers must still ensure that their workers are documented. As of 2023, there have been new attempts to further restrict the rights of immigrants in states like Florida, with passage of legislation (HB 1617/SB 1718) that, for example, criminalize assistance (e.g., providing shelter or transportation) to undocumented immigrants or those with expired visas, in addition to harming businesses with random checks and restricting access to healthcare via requiring hospitals to verify if Medicaid patients are in the U.S. legally (ACLU Florida, n.d.).

Given the increase of anti-immigration sentiments within the past 10 years largely targeting the Latinx community, remnants of strict immigration laws in states like Alabama, newer restrictive legislation in Florida, and the increasing teacher shortage, it is of utmost importance to better understand the lived experiences of Latinx teachers and how they navigate the education arena. Understanding these experiences has the possibility of creating more supportive environments in K-12 schools, debunking stereotypes, providing rich cultural accounts, humanizing the Latinx perspective, and fortifying the need for further exploration of the recruitment and retention of Latinx teachers.

While the literature surrounding the lived experiences of Latinx teachers in the United States is increasing (e.g., Colomer, 2014; Gomez, 2010; Flores, 2011; Gomez & Rodriguez, 2011; Kayi-Aydar, 2018; Soto Huerta, 2019), there is still much to be learned about Latinx teachers. There is a gap in the research regarding the lived experiences of Latina teachers both within and outside the classroom in order to cultivate agency and healing by way of sharing stories and experiences (e.g., stories from young adult fiction and personal life stories). The experiences of Latina teachers are especially pertinent given the increasingly hostile climate toward Latinx communities in the United States and the unique experiences with race and racism that people of Color experience in predominantly non-Latinx spaces such as the Deep South (i.e., in majority White or Black spaces). There is also a dearth of research that uses young adult literature (YAL) as counter-narratives to explore the experiences of Latinx teachers from different Latinx countries. We know that for there to be a meaningful transaction between the reader and text, an aesthetic approach is needed whereby the reader establishes a personal connection to the text via the emotional complexities inherent in the text's language and readers' lives (Rosenblatt, 1978). There is, however, scant research centering Latinas and the aesthetic approach to textual transactions, and how such an approach can take the form of a counter-narrative for individuals (like Latinas) whose life experiences have been marginalized. Literature is a vehicle that can aide in humanizing the experiences of Latinas, in addition to acting as a step toward normalizing the truth or counter-narratives that Latinas harbor. Thus, the purpose of this book is to explore the lived experiences of Latina teachers with five or more years of teaching experience, who have taught in the greater metropolitan area of Birmingham, Alabama. Young adult literature written by Latina authors and featuring Latina narrators have been used as a bridge to discuss the personal and schooling experiences of Latinas.

## Pathways Toward Discovery

We often treat people the way that we perceive them to be, thus, this book aims to share the lived experiences of Latina teachers to aid in reshaping the perceptions we have about Latinas who teach. The primary research questions that will guide this book include the following:

1. What perspectives do Latina teachers share about their personal and schooling lived experiences in the Deep South?
2. How do the teachers describe their lived experiences as related to young adult literature written by Latinas?
3. What can we learn from Latina teachers through their personal and schooling lived experiences?

## Conclusion

Rarely have Latina teachers been asked about their stories and experiences within and outside of the classroom in order to bridge understanding amongst themselves. The use of literature to guide such critical discussions with Latina teachers has also not been explored. Validation of the experiences of the Latina teachers featured in this book increased their agency and cultivation of healing. Just like teachers are encouraged to be active readers and writers to model skills and practices for their students, they must also become models of anti-racist pedagogy, which can begin by exploring their intracultural understanding. Glazier and Seo found that using multiple multicultural young adult books could help to establish "a global perspective, along with improving intercultural and intracultural understanding" (2005, as cited in Hayn, Kaplan, & Nolen, 2011, p. 178). Similarly, Latinx YAL spotlighted in this book helped establish a means to broaden the critical perspectives that Latina teachers had about their own and each other's lived experiences. Prior research indicates that there is still a need for "culturally efficacious teachers [that] understand how their ethnicity impacts student learning" (Bustos Flores, Riojas Clark, Claeys, & Villarreal, 2007, p. 64). There is also a need to bolster the support networks of Latina teachers (Ocasio, 2014). Further, we still need to move beyond an essentialized notion of what it means to be an "authentic" Latina and to interrupt narratives of authenticity (Flores & García, 2009). The research literature has not yet examined spaces for Latina teachers to explore their female Latinidad by way of using critical multicultural and Latinx YAL to share their lived experiences. This book explores such a space.

This book focuses on three female Latina teachers living in the Deep South, specifically the Greater Metropolitan Birmingham Area of Alabama. The geographic boundaries are, however, intended to focus on an area where limited research has been conducted on Latina teachers. Additionally, the study upon which the book is based took place over the course of three months, thereby putting constraints on the methodological approach of a narrative ethnography. It, however, relied on a short-term narrative ethnographic approach, with an intensive timeframe from which to conduct and be immersed with the Latina teachers. Finally, the original study inadvertently occurred during the midst of an unprecedented time in history, with a global pandemic (i.e., COVID-19) and a tumultuous presidential term and election that resulted in increased racial tensions/violence/awareness. These sociopolitical and health/ wellness factors undoubtedly affected the teachers' general sense of anxiety, albeit tinged with pleasure and relief of coming together to share experiences during a time when teachers (and the general public) were isolated.

## Organization of the Book

Chapter one, "Latina Teachers: Trenzas and Counter-Narratives," explores the literature surrounding the two primary frameworks from which the book and original study are based, that is, Latino/a Critical Race Theory (LatCrit) and Chicana/Latina Feminism. In addition, this chapter provides information about the literature surrounding testimonios, intersectionalities, hybrid identities, and young adult literature. Specifically, the chapter foregrounds the tenets and epistemological knowledges and trenzas that act as navigational tools for the inquiry and findings of the book and original study. These theoretical frameworks aided in disrupting dominant and traditional research paradigms by incorporating multiple cultural trenzas and "trenzas de identidades multiples/braids of multiple identities" (Godinez, 2006).

Chapter two, "Laying the Foundation: Background Information on the Original Study," provides a general overview of the methodology of the study from which the book is based, including information about the Latina teachers, how I collected data, and how the theoretical foundations of LatCrit and Chicana/Latina Feminism guided all aspects of the study and this book. Most importantly, I will illustrate how I centered a loving and nourishing gaze to interact with the Latina teachers, their lived experiences, and the young adult literature protagonists. Specifically, young adult literature texts were used to explore various Latinidades and bridge discussion about counter-stories and hybrid identities. Latinx literature themes such as "interdependence between generations" and privileging the "heritage ways of knowing and being" were examined (Alamillo, 2007). Additionally, ways in which the Latina teachers' experiences converged and diverged from each other and in contrast to the young adult literature protagonists were also centered and interrogated.

Chapter three, "Cuentos y Testimonios," also features three testimonios depicting the essence of the stories told by the three Latina teachers. The testimonios imbue muxerista portraiture, which centers asset-based "life-drawings" (Lawrence-Lighfoot, 2015, p. 5) of the teachers and my/the "portraitist's cultural intuition" (Flores, 2017, p. 2). I drew on my own Latina experiences and cultural intuition to identify recurring themes and findings by way of the teachers' cultural dichos/sayings, metaphors, and analogies. Additionally, the testimonios feature a multiplicity of Latina identities and experiential knowledges, as well as examples of where negotiations and resistance of nepantla (or in-between cultural spaces) intersected with racial tension, confusion, and assimilation.

Chapter four, "Cultivating the Experiences of Latina Teachers in the Deep South," explains and summarizes the key findings that emerged via themes that were based on the stories the Latina teachers shared. Specifically, how the Latina teachers' stories appeared to progressively voice a deepened understanding about their hybrid identities and "geography of selves" (Anzaldua, 2015). That is, they began to acknowledge how their experiences were like "diverse, bordering, and overlapping countries" (Anzaldua, 2015, p. 69). Even though the teachers could not readily name or use critically conscious vocabulary, their stories appeared to show how they navigated the cracks and gaps of nepantla, the in-between cultural worlds that would ultimately lead them toward a "hybrid consciousness that transcends the us versus them mentality of irreconcilable positions" (Anzaldua, 2015, p. 79).

Chapter five, "Y Ahora Que? What Can We Learn From Latina Teachers?," presents a review of the findings, implications, and recommendations for future research. A discussion of the three guiding research inquiries is reviewed. Implications for K-12 schooling and teacher education programs are also explored. Lastly, implications for further research in the areas of young adult literature texts to bridge critical conversations and leverage experiences between literary characters and teachers of Color, including Latina teachers, is examined.

· 1 ·

# LATINA TEACHERS: TRENZAS AND COUNTER-NARRATIVES

## Latina Teachers and Chicana/Latina Feminism

*Trenzas de mi pasado*
*Trenzas de mi herencia*
> *Historias y antepasados*
> *De mujeres resistentes y llenas de humildad.*
*Of women who forsook*
*Dreams of their future*
> *Who followed their husbands yet*
> *Advocated for their hijas.*[1]

The cultural trenzas of mi pasado (braids of my past), rich with ancestral history and desire, anchored my personal ties to this book. In the introduction of the book, I described how my sense of being othered led me to research how Latina teachers in the Deep South navigate their professional and personal spaces via the use of young adult literature (YAL) written by Latina authors. Such multicultural literature can acknowledge and critically examine multiple and alternative ways of growing up American as a Latinx, explore equity issues and power structures, and can "amplify voices of people who have been left out of both U.S. and Latinx canons, and collectively question and engage with key stereotypes of U.S. literature and culture" (Garcia, 2017, p. 117; Cai, 2002).

In this chapter, I will describe how specific theoretical frameworks and ways of thinking guided the strands of epistemological trenzas that fortified this

| | | |
|---|---|---|
| | LatCrit in Education | Centers race and racism<br>Challenges dominant ideologies (e.g., deficit perspectives)<br>Commits to social justice<br>Values experiential/first-hand knowledge<br>Adopts interdisciplinary perspectives |
| | Chicana/Latina Feminism in Education | Centers Latina voices and experiences<br>Challenges traditional forms of knowledge<br>Commits to anti-oppressive, social justice approach<br>Values multiplicity of Latina identities |
| | Multicultural and Latinx Young Adult Literature | Centers non-dominant voices<br>Challenges oppressive factors<br>Commits to intersectionalities<br>Values equity |

Figure 1: *Conceptual Trenzas of the Book*

book. Specifically, I will explain how Latino/a Critical Race Theory (LatCrit) in education contextualized the intersectionalities of various forms of subordination and counter-stories that were considered in order to better understand Latina teachers and their Latinidad. I will also explain how testimonios and Chicana/Latina Feminism further intensified an exploration of intersectionalities and hybrid identities by examining the ancestral strength that came from mujeres resistentes within the cultural backgrounds of the Latina teachers. Lastly, I will review how Latinx young adult literature has provided an optimal way to bridge counter-stories and hybrid identities, in addition to providing a platform to discuss the Latina teachers' personal experiences. Figure one provides a summary of the trenzas/braids that undergird the theoretical and epistemological strands of this book.

## Latino/A Critical Race Theory (LatCrit)

LatCrit originated from Critical Race Theory (CRT). According to Delgado (1995):

> Critical Race Theory begins with a number of basic insights. One is that racism is normal, not aberrant, in American society. Because racism is an ingrained feature of our landscape, it looks ordinary and natural to persons in the culture. Formal equal

opportunity rules and laws that insist on treating Black and whites (for example) alike, can thus remedy only the more extreme and shocking sorts of injustice[.] Formal equality can do little about the business-as-usual forms of racism that people of color confront every day and that account for much misery, alienation, and despair (p. xiv).

Thus, CRT provides a means to critique racism within laws and societal norms, in addition to focusing on "everyday racism" that consists of "mundane practices . . . infused with some degree of unconscious racial mal-intent," including microaggressions that can be "subtle, automatic, non-verbal exchanges that are seen as derogatory slights by persons of color" (Lynn & Parker, 2006, p. 260). CRT theorists maintain that race is based primarily on social constructions that "society invents, manipulates, or retires when convenient" (Delgado & Stefancic, 2001, p. 7). Of particular concern, is how the dominant White society "racializes different minority groups at different times" and for different purposes, based on shifting stereotypes aimed at portraying groups of people in docile, complacent, or violent and aggressive ways (Delgado & Stefancic, 2001, p. 8).

Both LatCrit and CRT emerged from the effort of legal scholars of color to address and critique the role of racism within the American legal system and societal norms (Matsuda, 1991). Four of the primary and overlapping functions of LatCrit are to:

- produce knowledge relative to understanding Latinxs and the law;
- advance transformation relative to applicability and social conditions leading to praxis or action;
- highlight the experiences of Latinxs by way of exploring struggles, including a rejection of unidimensional views of Latinxs; and
- actively cultivate a community of scholars committed to collaborating toward social action (Valdes, 1997, pp. 1093–1094).

The four functions seek to resist essentialism of the Latinx community and embrace intersectionality, much like this book looks at the racialized and hybrid identities of Latinx teachers via their lived experiences and the experiences of Latina female characters in three young adult literature texts. Among some of the concepts that LatCrit highlights are how Latinxs can internalize and even embrace dominant assimilationist norms in self-harming ways that fuel the othering of Latinxs (Valdes, 1997). Latinxs, for example, have been dehumanized and reduced to a singular homogenous group viewed as a threat to America's economy, social services, and safety (Arce, 2019; Korte & Gomez, 2018; Scott, 2019). Language such as "illegal aliens," "animals," "rapists," and "bad hombres" (Arce, 2019; Korte & Gomez, 2018; Scott, 2019) aid in perpetuating violence against Latinxs – language, in essence, is used as a weapon . . . a linguistic and narrative weapon that incites emotional and physical violence. Such language, as used as a weapon of the colonizer, could have negative repercussions on the self-narratives that Latinx teachers use to define themselves and guide their teaching decisions.

Solorzano and Yosso (2001) posited five themes that undergird a CRT (and LatCrit) in education, as listed below:

- centering race and racism,
- challenging dominant ideologies such as deficit perspectives,
- committing to social justice,
- valuing experiential and first-hand knowledge, and
- adopting an interdisciplinary perspective.

Stories and counter-stories provide salient methods for critical race theorists to highlight multiple perspectives, thereby projecting an understanding of how race is viewed and experienced in America (Delgado & Stefancic, 2001). CRT allows the researcher to make "a deliberate appearance in his or her work" (Ladson-Billings, 2000, p. 272). LatCrit, in particular, uses narrative counter-storytelling to examine the ways in which race and racism specifically affect the Latinx population. For example, Solorzano and Yosso (2001) explicitly highlighted how LatCrit intersects with different types of subordination like gender and sexism when they narrated an experience about a Latina scholar being racialized and sexualized in their counter-story (p. 484). They also described being silenced, yet using "silenced voices" (p. 486) as narratives that centered and advanced the actions of people and students of Color by constructing these narratives as sources of strength, rather than deficits. In this book, stories, counter-stories, and narrative accounts guide the development and analysis of the testimonios, which are based on experiences that the Latina teachers shared, including my own.

Osorio (2018) stressed that LatCrit relies on experiences unique to the Latinx community to better understand the lived realities of Latinxs. Her research highlighted how her Latinx students used their borderstories to connect the political climate to the increased amount of unaccompanied immigrant children entering the U.S. Thus, aspects such as immigration and language diversity were centered as part of employing a LatCrit theoretical framework. Valdes (1997) underscored such intersections by delineating, among other functions, how Lat-Crit also incorporates the sustenance of knowledge by voices that have been his-torically silenced, in addition to the reinforcement of community and solidarity via research that aids in bringing people together against dominant discourses.

CRT challenges assumptions that schooling is neutral and operates in the same way for every student, in addition to resisting and questioning notions like meritocracy and color-neutrality, which falsely promulgate that hard work alone leads to success and everyone should be viewed the same no matter their racialized (or skin color) experiences (Perez-Huber, 2010). LatCrit extends CRT to center how the pan-ethnic Latinx community experiences structural racism and intersections between class, gender, and sexuality, in addition to issues related to immigration, culture, and language (Hernandez-Truyol, 1997; Sol-orzano & Delgado Bernal, 2001). Thus, LatCrit allows for the examination of the lived experiences of Latinx individuals by centering the specific forms of oppression and marginalization that they experience. This book relies on Lat-Crit to foreground how counter-stories and experiential knowledge are inextri-cably linked to exploring the complex and multifaceted traits that humanize and authenticate the experiences of the Latina teachers. It explores how the life experiences of the Latina teachers, in addition to their levels of assimilation and acculturation, and daily toll of navigating within a structurally racist and oppressive system of schooling, have impacted the perspectives and criticality they incorporate into their classrooms. More broadly, the study upon which the book is based occurred in Alabama, a state with a hostile racial history, where the voices and bodies of people of Color have been silenced, policed, and brutalized. The literature regarding CRT and LatCrit in education also emphasizes how the fluidity and complexity of internalized racism and racial microaggressions negatively affect the education of teachers and students of Color (Kohli, 2014). By inviting Latina teachers who represent several Lat-inx communities, including young adult literature representative of Mexico, Guatemala, and the Dominican Republic, and incorporating cultural prac-tices that honor various forms of Latinidad (e.g., sharing food and reflecting on experiences via visual/art journals at the book gatherings), this book enacts principles that are aligned with LatCrit. Like LatCrit, testimonio is marked by its objective to highlight varying perspectives and call for subsequent action (Reyes & Rodriguez, 2012). This book utilizes testimonios that are anchored by LatCrit and Chicana/Latina Feminism to explore and celebrate the valued experiences of Latina teachers.

## Chicana/Latina Feminism and Testimonios

Testimonio and Chicana/Latina Feminism center the Latina and her lived experiences. Further, Chicana/Latina Feminism "expose[s] the multi-layered 'inner faces' [of Latinas], attempting to confront and oust the internalized oppression embedded in them, and remake anew both inner and outer faces" (Anzaldúa, 1990). Chicana/Latina Feminism situates the intuitive and ancestral voices of our mothers, grandmothers, great grandmothers, aunts, great-aunts, and sisters to break the silences that have constrained and marginalized our voices. It foregrounds the intersections between race, class, gender, and sexuality – not solely gender (Delgado Bernal, 1998).

Delgado Bernal's (1998) seminal article entitled, "Using a Chicana Feminist Epistemology in Educational Research" outlined an epistemological foundation informed by Chicana feminism to critically examine notions of researcher objectivity and a universal source of knowledge. She highlighted how traditional educational research and feminist scholarship failed to offer paradigms that examined the lives of Chicanas, and bolstered the need for a Chicana feminist epistemology that would situate Chicanas as "agents of knowledge who participate in intellectual discourse that links experience, research, community, and social change" (Delgado Bernal, 1998, p. 559). Delgado Bernal (1998) then used the work of Strauss and Corbin (as cited in Delgado Bernal, 1998, pp. 561–563) to expand on four sources of cultural intuition or what she described as the distinct viewpoints that Chicana researchers bring to research. More specifically, cultural intuition consists of personal experience, professional experience, existing literature on a topic, and the analytic research process. Delgado Bernal (1998) described personal experience as not only comprising the background every researcher brings to the research process, but also encompassing community knowledge and memory of past traumas of conquest and segregation, in addition to the collective experiences and ancestral wisdom that influence the personal experiences of Chicanas. Professional experience encompasses the amount of accumulated experiences that can contribute to an overall richer knowledge brought to the research process. Lastly, Delgado Bernal (1998) extended Strauss and Corbin's notion of analytical research process by advocating for a Chicana feminist epistemology composed of an interactive data analysis process that included Chicana research participants. Existing literature includes traditional literature, but also covers other types of literature, including personal documents, descriptive writings like newspaper articles, and biographies (i.e., literature meant to sensitize, shape, and contextualize what to look for in data or the overall circumstances of what is being studied). This book seeks to incorporate a Chicana feminist epistemology by extending Delgado Bernal's concept of cultural intuition to include Latina teachers representative of multiple hybrid and intersecting identities, from different parts of the Latino diaspora, yet residing in the Greater Birmingham Metropolitan Area of Alabama.

Interestingly, Gloria Anzaldúa (2015) wrote about how the places in which she lived impacted her psyche and how she negotiated the definitions and concepts of otherness that encompassed her multiplicity of identities. She described how "our bodies are geographies of selves made up of diverse, bordering, and overlapping countries" (p. 69). More importantly, she described how identities are relational to the ways we interact with each other and our environments.

> As our bodies interact with internal and external, real and virtual, past and present environments, people, and objects around us, we weave [tejemos] and are woven into, our identities. Identity as consciously and unconsciously created, is always in process – self interacting with different communities and worlds (Anzaldua, 2015, p. 69).

Anzaldúa (2015) further expanded on the concept of geography of self by describing how we each negotiate the borders within which our bodies interact – such negotiation results in mestizaje or a new type of identity, a new mestiza. Anzaldúa (1987) described a mestiza as being in transition, facing the challenge of a "mixed breed," undergoing a "struggle of borders, an inner war" (p. 100). She emphasized that a new mestiza consciousness took place "underground – subconsciously" and "where the possibility of uniting all that is separate occurs" (Anzaldúa, 1987, p. 101). Thus, the mestiza lives between more than one culture, however, the new mestiza has started developing "a tolerance for contradictions, a tolerance for ambiguity . . . she learns to juggle cultures" (Anzaldúa, 1987, p. 101) and lives between the cracks and gaps, in nepantla (Anzaldúa, 2015, p. 71). Nepantla comprises places and spaces of dissonance, clash, grind, asymmetry (Anzaldúa, 2015). To live within this state of nepantla, a state of liminality, is to be in a transitional space where individuals can be "caught in the midst of denying their projected/assumed" identity(ies) (Anzaldúa, 2015, p. 56). Mestizaje and nepantla resist binaries and categories of either/or (e.g., male/female, black/white, rich/poor) and emphasize, for example, the negotiation among ethnic groups and "cultural mixtures" (Anzaldúa, 2015, p. 73).

In fact, much like the Latina teachers in this book explored, Anzaldúa (2015) illuminated how Latinxs are in conocimiento y desconocimiento [knowledge and ignorance] of their unique experiences and histories, in addition to living "entremedios [in between] in a tense balance with each other and with other groups ... in collisions and conflicts with those bearing different views – [they] perpetuate mental and emotional violence against each other" (p. 73). Living and navigating within the gaps of nepantla, including interracial and intra-racial conflict, however, provides access to "experiences and abilities that can catapult [Latinxs] into creating innovative, inclusive identities" (Anzaldúa, 2015, p. 73). She advocated for identifying the common, yet different experiences that comprise Latinxs, while also honoring what makes us diverse. One specific route toward navigating nepantla and resisting binaries of us/them is via an identity narrative of "nos/otras" or "us"/"others" (i.e., female others), which Anzaldúa (2015) described as "an identity born of negotiating the cracks between worlds, nos/otras accommodates contradictory identities and social positions, creating a hybrid consciousness that transcends the us versus them mentality of irreconcilable positions, blurring the boundary between us and others" (p. 79). Most importantly, she emphasized that although it is difficult and often painful, intimacy and closeness can begin to close the gaps between us/them. The nos/otras identity, for instance, aims to disrupt dominant racial and identity categories by embracing a hybrid consciousness that nurtures "cultural sensitivities to difference" (Anzaldúa, 2015, p. 81).

Anzaldua's work fortifies one of the main trenzas of this book by providing the foundation about hybrid identities and how Latinas embody a mestizaje and multiplicity of identities that exist in nepantla (or the in-between spaces of our lives). Her work established hope of conocimiento – the foundation to be seen because, not in spite of, our complex Latina identities, even while living in a divisive state like Alabama. This foundational trenza seamlessly intertwines with the use of testimonios as a source of narrative storytelling in this book.

The Latina Feminist Group (2001) turned to testimonio and an exploration of feminist Latinidades after determining that "the national-ethnic identity categories did not encompass the actual diversity of Latinas, as they ignored difference in class backgrounds, religious traditions, sexual preferences, races, ages, cultural experiences, regional variations, and women of mixed or Native American heritage" (p. 11). Originally used in Latin American literature, oral history, and human rights advocacy (Menchu, 1984), Chicanas and Latinas have used testimonio to expose violence against and build solidarity among Latinas (Anzaldúa, 1990; Moraga & Anzaldúa, 1983; Delgado Bernal, Burciaga, & Flores Carmona, 2012). In education, testimonio has been utilized as methodology, pedagogy, counter-narratives, and forms of social activism. It "challenges objectivity by situating the individual in communion with a collective experience marked by marginalization, oppression, or resistance" (Delgado Bernal et al., 2012, p. 363). Further, testimonio intentionally affirms, empowers, and allows a narrator to describe experiences that are transformational and liberating by way of sharing the experience. In turn, the testimonio may become political by way of heightening the readers' awareness (Reyes & Rodriguez, 2012).

Testimonio as a form of methodology by and about Latinas has been well documented in the research literature (Delgado Bernal et al., 2012; Menchu, 1984; Reyes & Rodriguez, 2012). For example, Perez Huber (2009, 2010) centered testimonio as a methodology and methodological strategy to disrupt knowledge-making in academia by employing LatCrit to undergird the testimonios of undocumented and U.S.-born Chicana university students. Brabeck (2003) relied on testimonio as an alternative methodology to disrupt overrepresentation of Whiteness within feminist methodological studies. Ochoa (2016) utilized a testimonio methodological approach to conduct and analyze testimonio interviews of undocumented immigrants, aimed at depicting narratives of survival and critiquing the immigration system in the United States.

Testimonios have also been engaged as a methodological approach to participate in critical dialogue and praxis. Additionally, testimonios have been employed in an epistemological and theoretical manner to explore and embrace a multiplicity of voices and identities via collective testimonios by and about Latinas. For instance, Martinez (2017) employed testimonio as methodology, epistemology, and praxis to explore the leadership experiences of four Latina scholars by highlighting critical dialogue representative of each scholar. Similarly, Saavedra and Perez (2012) employed testimonio to examine their own research and teaching, as inspired by Chicana and Black feminisms. They described their relationship as amigas and colegas (friends and colleagues) who have "foster[ed] resistance and strength in [their] academic and life journeys" (p. 431). They each took up space, bearing witness to each other, to dialogue about their theoretical frameworks, shifting identities, and critical examination of multiculturalism. Martinez-Roldan and Quinones (2016) also used testimonios as methodology and narrative development to explore their experiences surrounding English usage that impacted their research scholarship and academic careers. They emphasized the need to tell their stories and develop "mentoring networks . . . [to] cultivate solidarity as a means of thriving in the academy" (p. 151).

The importance of creating spaces for Latinas to share their experiences and learn from each other was also explored by Flores and García (2009), who employed testimonio to theorize from their experiences, "to produce new knowledge, recognition, and forms of empowerment" (p. 156). In the article, they each claimed space to share their critical self-reflections of being Latina scholars in predominantly White institutions. They describe the creation of a Latinas Telling Testimonios group that they initiated to intentionally create a space for Latinas "to learn from each other's differences and to theorize the complexities of our communities" (p. 156). Engaging in pláticas and sharing vulnerable testimonios highlighted the Latinas' lived experiences and the diverse complexities of their experiences. The testimonios Flores and García describe disrupted the notion of an essentialized Latina and problematized the notion of Latina authenticity, thereby reinforcing the need for Latina spaces to disrupt silences and talk "cara a cara, de corazon a corazon [face to face, heart to heart]" (p. 170).

Testimonios also reinforce pedagogy as a means to increase criticality (Flores Carmona & Luciano, 2014). Espino, Muñoz, and Marquez Kiyama (2010) presented their personal narratives via testimonios as a form of cultural survival that exposed their encounters with race, gender, and class as doctoral students. They wove a collective testimonio that culminated in a sisterhood of sustenance during their graduate schooling experience. This element of weaving was contextualized as a braid of their multiple identities, or trenzas de identidades multiples (Godinez, 2006). The authors were cognizant, however, of the risk of essentializing their experiences through their testimonios.

Montoya (1994) utilized autobiographical narrative to explore the unbraiding of stories that revealed how counter-stories resist "cultural and linguistic domination through personal and collective redefinition" (p. 185). Montoya (1994) used hair-braids (i.e., trenzas) as a metaphor representing presentability to the outside Anglo world and as a means to depict the sociocultural differences and circumstances between her Latinx family and wealthier Anglo classmates at her Catholic school. She extended the metaphor of trenzas to include mascaras/masks that represented forms of assimilation such as lack of an English accent and limited Spanish language use, learned from her parents as a defense against racism. Montoya (1994) described how assimilation and belonging to a higher socioeconomic class than one's family can lead to isolation, estrangement, and resentment about the "cultural costs" (p. 192) that result from academic and economic successes (i.e., accusations of purposely losing cultural attributes). She wrote that when Latinas are told that they don't seem Latina, "such comments, when made by Anglos, imply that we have risen above our group. We are special, better, acceptable. When made by Latinos, however, the question carries an innuendo of cultural betrayal and the threat of cultural excommunication." (Montoya, 1994, p. 192). Montoya (1994) also emphasized the need for research about Latinas' bicultural identities to "transform self-understanding and reclaim for all Latinas the right to define ourselves and to reject unidimensional interpretations of our personal and collective experience" (p. 206). This autobiographical exploration included the use of Spanish and English to convey counter-stories of wisdom and culture.

Godinez (2006) also incorporated trenzas by way of a multimethodological research approach that wove trenzas of identities, qualitative research, and critical consciousness in what she defined as trenzas y mestizaje. Godinez (2006) crafted a "looking prism" (p. 26) where multiple intersectionalities were essential to explain the ways in which "gender, race/ethnicity, class, and sexuality intersect in shaping structural, political, and representational dimensions within women of color lives" (p. 27), and specifically, the lives of the young Mexicanas she studied. In reworking Montoya's (1994) concept of trenzas, Godinez (2006) theorized pláticas and pláticas y encuentros (dialogue and happenings) as conversations whereby she interviewed participants and included her researcher voice to "gather family and cultural knowledge through communication of thoughts, memories, ambiguities, and new interpretations" (p. 30). Godinez's (2006) study ultimately highlighted how spirituality was interwoven throughout the responses of the young high-school aged Mexican participants. Specifically, her study illuminated how spirituality was brought forth via cultural and familial consejos and educación (advice and daily teachings) from home, which was essentially how the Mexicanas formed their sense of Mexicanness (Godinez, 2006, p. 32)

This theoretical framework section on Chicana/Latina Feminism and testimonios centers the dynamic, unique, and complex Latina identities and multiplicities in order to foreground aspects such as how our bodies comprise the fissures, cracks, nepantla, and trenzas of our lived experiences. Latinx young adult literature (featuring Latina protagonists) also embodies the depth and centrality that Chicana/Latina Feminism promulgates. Below is a synopsis of how multicultural and Latinx young adult literature facilitates critical reflection that guides critical dialogue about Latinidad in this book. The information below centers how young adult literature was used as a conceptual framework to facilitate creative reflection, self-affirmation, and intracultural understanding among the Latina teachers.

# Young Adult Literature (YAL) Written by Latinas

Stories humanize us. They emphasize our differences in ways that can ultimately bring us closer together. They allow us to see how the world looks from
behind someone else's spectacles. They challenge us to wipe off our own lenses
and ask, "Could I have been overlooking something all along?" (Delgado, 1989,
p. 2440). Delgado (1989) highlighted the nature of reality as ever-changing,
evolving, and broadening via conversations and dialogue. He explained that
"racial and class-based isolation prevents the hearing of diverse stories and
counterstories" (Delgado, 1989, p. 2439). Thus, while stories and counter-stories
have the power to humanize, they also act as a means to challenge individual realities. More specifically, listening and telling various counter-stories (or
versions of reality) aid in creating "a rich tapestry of conversation, of stories"
(Delgado, 1989, p. 2439), so that the same dominant or stock stories representing the status quo (or mainstream, White stories) do not perpetuate a sole
view of reality. Hughes-Hassell (2013), for example, emphasized the use of multicultural young adult literature (YAL) as counter-stories to dominant stories
and stereotypes about indigenous communities and people of color. She highlighted how counter-stories can help the reader understand that their beliefs
may be inaccurate. Most importantly, Hughes-Hassell stressed the importance
of the insight that readers of color (including indigenous ones) gain about their
own "racial, ethnic, or cultural background" by reading stories about characters
of color in multicultural YAL (p. 219). Such insights, Hughes-Hassell stressed,
aid in affirming the readers' own racial and ethnic identities.

Much like counter-stories, YAL can provide an opportunity to engage
in critical reflection and critical dialogue of the intricacies that, for example,
comprise complex Latina characters from diverse backgrounds. Literature can
help readers confront difficult truths about injustices, in addition to helping
the reader better understand herself (Wolk, 2009). Additionally, multicultural
YAL can give voice to otherwise unheard voices, challenge the notion of a
singular story about diverse experiences, and present characters with complex racial and ethnic identities that help readers of color "gain insight to how
other [readers] who share" similar "racial, ethnic, or cultural backgrounds have
affirmed their own identities" (Hughes-Hassell, 2013, p. 219).

By making personal connections to Latina characters and interacting
with the characters' multifaceted perspectives, the Latina teachers featured in
this book relied on their own narratives to expand upon cultural notions of

Latinidad. YAL portrays characters as individuals searching for their genuine selves, as constantly evolving, and attempting to break free of being considered an outsider. "To be 'other' is to not belong but, instead, to be outcast. Thus, to see oneself in the pages of a young adult book is to receive the reassurance that one is not alone after all, not other, not alien but, instead, a viable part of a larger community of beings who share a common humanity" (YALSA, 2008). Rudine Sims Bishop (1990) eloquently stated:

> Books are sometimes windows, offering views of worlds that may be real or imagined, familiar or strange. These windows are also sliding glass doors, and readers have only to walk through in imagination to become part of whatever world has been created or recreated by the author. When lighting conditions are just right, however, a window can also be a mirror. Literature transforms human experience and reflects it back to us, and in that reflection we can see our own lives and experiences as part of the larger human experience. Reading, then, becomes a means of self-affirmation, and readers often seek their mirrors in books (para. 1).

The following are examples of other researchers who centered the use of YAL to emphasize counter-storytelling by or for Latinxs. García and Gaddes (2012) used critical reading and mentor texts via culturally relevant literature with Latina adolescents to write stories that relied on their cultural and linguistic funds of knowledge (González, Moll, & Amanti, 2005). García and Gaddes relied on Louise Rosenblatt's (1978) transactional literary theory to focus on how a text and its reader "are involved in a nonlinear relationship of meaning making at a particular time and place" (p. 146). Using culturally relevant texts (e.g., short stories, novels, poems) written by Latina authors allowed their Latina adolescent writers to use their personal experiences when engaging with and interpreting the mentor texts. García and Gaddes used the notion of cultural authenticity to select the mentor texts used in their study. They concentrated on and acknowledged the intertwined threads of complexity that burden how society defines cultural authenticity. The goal of the mentor texts was to help the Latina writers realize that their experiences and struggles were shared by other Latinas, and to provide life strategies from the characters in the texts. Similarly, the study upon which this book is based relied on YAL to showcase various Latina characters with intersecting identities, so that the Latina teachers could experience varying versions of Latinidad, thereby mirroring and expanding on their own lived experiences.

Sonia Alejandra Rodriguez (2018) used Gloria Anzaldúa's (2002) notion of *conocimiento* narratives as a way to connect one YAL text to Chicanas/Latinas via a literary space where Chicana/Latina readers could see themselves. She examined a YAL text written by a Latina author that challenged dominant narratives and highlighted how such an examination could lead to empowerment. She centered the Latina protagonist's experiences as sources of knowledge that could challenge the forms of oppression she faced in the book, thereby highlighting how reading books can have the potential for healing. In her article, she described how *conocimiento* narratives can be used to examine alternative knowledges as depicted by children's books and YAL. She summarized Anzaldua's (2002) seven stages of *conocimiento* as *el arrebato* (a break), nepantla (in-between space), Coatlicue state of despair, the call or a compromise, rejoining Coyolxauhqui (piecing together), the blow up or conflict of realities, and a shifting of realities. Anzaldúa (2002) explained that the stages and process of *conocimiento* are fluid, not linear. Rodriguez described how the protagonist in her featured YAL text moved through the stages of *conocimiento* in a nonlinear fashion to challenge "discriminatory narratives" that occurred at school by relying on her personal knowledges (e.g., friends, community, culture). Though Rodriguez (2018) did not use participants to discuss or compare their lives with the life of the main character of the book she analyzed, the study from which this book is based relied on mentor YAL texts as a means to create a space where Latina teachers examined their lives in relation to the Latina protagonists in the texts. In doing so, the Latina teachers discussed how the protagonists, and consequently themselves, navigated oppressive narratives.

Marilisa Jimenez García (2018) focused on how current Latinx YAL authors use YAL to explore different variations of social justice by way of using counter-storytelling. García focused on two YAL texts to provide an example of how Latinx writers challenge YAL textual norms. These foci highlighted two character tropes, the rebellious adolescent and a young adult working through trauma and described how these tropes are treated differently in Latinx YAL. The Latinx protagonists, García contended, resist forms of colonial oppression through their activism in the YAL. Additionally, García underscored how Latinx YAL emphasizes family relationships and how these relationships aid in the Latinx protagonist's journey rather than separating from the adolescent's journey. García described the adults in the two texts she discussed as being "just as limited and subjugated as the young people, if not more so" (p. 237). She examined how Latinx YAL include multiple and alternative ways of growing up American as a Latinx.

Narratives in Latinx YAL can center the perspectives of empowered female protagonists, thereby centering the asset-based approaches of LatCrit and Chicana/Latina Feminism. In fact, Rodriguez (2019) described Latinas in three

Latinx texts she examined as using "creativity and imagination to challenge and transform the different forms of violence they experience[d] in their lives" (p. 9). Such texts also foreground Latina protagonists who "contend with the gendered expectations of dominant white society but must also navigate the traditional, and often religious, gendered expectations of their Latinx culture" (Rodriguez, 2019, p. 9). Thus, Latinx YAL can center Latina protagonists who utilize creativity and curiosity that lead to their healing.

## Conclusion

This chapter focused on prior research regarding the conceptual trenzas of the theoretical frameworks from which the book and original study are centered. Specifically, LatCrit in Education, Chicana/Latina Feminism, and multicultural and Latinx young adult literature with a social justice focus. All of these frameworks center the unique complexities and multiple intersectionalities that abound in the lived experiences of Latinxs in the United States (e.g., how language intersects with perceived intelligence in schools, how one's body may clash with socially acceptable and normalized notions of beauty). Further, these frameworks center experiential knowledges like truth-narratives or counter-stories and cultural intuition based on ancestral knowledge and traditional forms of research.

The following chapter focuses on the methodology from which the original study was based. I describe the research methodology of the study, including information about the Latina teacher participants, the data collection and analysis, and how the two dominant theoretical frameworks of LatCrit and Chicana/Latina Feminism guided the study.

## Note

1 Literal Translation:
Braids of my past
Braids of my heritage
   Histories and ancestors
   Of resistant women full of humility
Of women who forsook
Dreams of their future
   Who followed their husbands yet
   Advocated for their daughters.

# LAYING THE FOUNDATION: BACKGROUND INFORMATION ON THE ORIGINAL STUDY

This book features the outcomes of a study that employed a narrative ethnographic approach, described below, that relied on testimonios to illustrate the narratives and counter-narratives of three Latina teachers, with the purpose of exploring the experiences of an under-represented group of educators in spaces where they are the minority (Delgado Bernal et al., 2012, p. 364). These testimonios were based on written and visual representations of the teachers' narratives. Young adult literature written by Latinas and depicting different Latinx cultures were used to unpack the narratives and assumptions the teachers had of themselves and each other by examining Latina characters that represented similar and different perspectives of Latinidad. This chapter focuses on general information relative to the overall study, including information about the Latina teacher participants and the collection and analysis of data. I have purposely included information surrounding the methodology of the original study, since the methodological approaches underpinning the study speak to the importance of centering the lives of Latinas (i.e., within and beyond the realm of critical and creative forms of research).

Narrative ethnography was essential for the qualitative study to explore how culture intersected with the Latina teachers' identities, experiences, and perspectives. This type of ethnography allowed for descriptive questions and responses aimed at understanding and interpreting the cultural meanings about the experiences and realities of the Latina teachers, to include examining places of disruption and discontinuity among the experiences and realities shared by the teachers during the study. Narrative ethnography was used as "an approach that renders explicit the relationships formed between [the] ethnographer and [participant] ... to create a world of shared intersubjectivity" (Tedlock, 1991, p. 70). I relied on such intersubjectivity by focusing on the stories that were told by the Latina teachers, which led me to identify themes that were repeated or based on "illuminating metaphors" (Lawrence-Lightfoot & Davis, 1997, p. 185). These stories became progressively more intimate, with convergent and sometimes dissonant threads, all of which led me to develop creative narratives or testimonios birthed from my own personal experiences and the trenzas of the Latina teachers' stories.

The study upon which this book is based explored the experiences of an under-represented group of educators living and working in predominantly non-Latinx spaces. Young adult literature (YAL) written by Latina authors and depicting three different Latinx cultures (i.e., from the Dominican Republic, Guatemala, and Mexico), and the intersectionalities between these Latinx cultures and American culture, were used to critically examine the Latina characters and reflect on the Latina teachers' own individual narratives and notions of Latinidad. The testimonios were a result of a pre- and post questionnaire, three individual in-depth conversations, three focus group book pláticas, altered books/artistic artifacts, and ethnographic field notes. Specifically, the YAL was discussed during three book pláticas, each occurring roughly three to four weeks after the teachers had read each book. During the individual interviews and book pláticas, the Latina teachers were encouraged to share personal and schooling information relative to each of their varied and complex cultural heritages and lived experiences, including (but not limited to) their relationships and identities with their language(s), their sense of nationality, and their country and/or citizenship of birth.

The research/inquiry questions for the original study aimed to discover the concepts that comprised the culture of Latina teachers from their insider perspective and experiences, rather than pre-defining what they reported based on predominant cultural norms. For example, rather than answering narrow and specific research questions about ways YAL could impact the teachers' level of intracultural understanding, I suspended the quest to answer any one specific outcome. Instead, I employed Spradley's (2016) approach to ethnographic research and focused on "what my informants know about their culture that I can discover" (p. 30). The research questions were as follows:

1. What perspectives do Latina teachers share about their personal and schooling lived experiences in the Deep South?
2. How do the teachers describe their lived experiences as related to young adult literature written by Latinas?
3. What can we learn from Latina teachers through their personal and schooling lived experiences?

I relied on LatCrit to explore and challenge elements of racism unique to the Latinx community, such as immigration status, ethnicity, culture, and language. Chicana/Latina Feminism also guided the critical dialogue during the book pláticas by placing the Latina experiences of the characters and teacher participants as central to the YAL. I relied on cultural intuition (Delgado Bernal, 1998; Monzó, 2015) to braid my own lived experiences as a Puerto Rican mother, daughter, teacher, and teacher educator to both of these overarching theoretical frameworks in order to build the study, as a means to create connections and deepen understandings about Latinidad and Latina identities. The lived experiences of the Latina teachers were also braided into the frame of the study via testimonios imbued with muxerista portraiture. Muxerista portraiture fuses Lawrence-Lightfoot's (2015) methodological portraiture approach of "life-drawing(s)" or engaging with a participant like an artist creating a portrait, and centers Chicana/Latina Feminism by focusing on the Latina participants' realities, intersectionalities, and lived experiences (Flores, 2017b). My intention in using the aforementioned frameworks and methodological approaches was to shed light on the Latinas' lived experiences via a loving gaze focused on genuinely seeing them – that is, with all of their complex intersectionalities and attributes, while being mindful not to essentialize the experiences as being representative of all Latina teachers or Latina teachers in the Deep South. Thus, the frameworks aided in understanding and nourishing nosotras/Latinas, especially given the predominantly non-Latinx situational space in which the study was conducted.

## Latina Teacher Participant-Collaborators

Given the lack of research on Latina teachers in the Deep South, the study took place in the Greater Birmingham Metropolitan Area of Alabama. This area falls within one major county, Jefferson County, where there are twelve independent school districts, with the largest comprising 58 schools and the smallest containing three schools (National Center for Education Statistics, n.d.). The large number of school districts within one main county is representative of Birmingham's complicated racial history and segregation laws. In fact, during the 2018–2019 school year, another local city was attempting to secede from the largest school district. This secession, however, was halted (though not closed) after a federal appeals court determined racial motives that impeded an existing desegregation order (i.e., all of the county schools remain under a 1965 and 1971 desegregation order to ensure racial balance and minimize discriminatory practices) (Faulk, 2019).

## Selection Criteria and Demographics of Research Participants

Selection criteria for this study consisted of the following: Latina cultural identity, at least five years of teaching experience, and currently teaching within the Greater Birmingham Metropolitan Area. Three Latina teachers with five or more years of teaching experience were recruited via purposeful and snowball sampling (Creswell & Poth, 2018). The rationale for selecting secondary education teachers was the likelihood that they could use the multicultural and Latinx young adult literature from this study in their own classrooms. In addition, the rationale for selecting teachers with five or more years of teaching experience was based on national teacher attrition whereby 40–50 % of new teachers leave the profession within the first five years of their teaching careers (Ingersoll, 2003, 2012). While the sole focus on female Latina teachers was intentional, this focus limited the transferability of findings to the more general population of Latinx teachers, including those identifying as male or gender fluid, subject content areas other than Spanish, and grade levels outside high school.

At the time of the study, the collaborators were aged 57, 55, and 39. Consuelo was married with two children, a son and daughter. Consuelo was born in Texas but lived in Alabama for 20 years and taught middle and high school Spanish for 19 years. Lucero was born in Venezuela, was widowed with no children, had lived in Alabama for 18 years, and had 25 years of teaching experience. Mercedes was born in Puerto Rico, was unmarried with no children, had lived in Alabama for 16 years, and had 13 years of teaching experience.

Without prodding or direction, the three teacher collaborators in this study selected the pseudonyms for themselves based on family nicknames given by a

parent or ancestral names from their families. In this study all three collaborators self-identified themselves in different nuanced ways to express their *Latinidad*. While they all indicated being Latina, when asked to explicitly self-identify
in an informal questionnaire, one identified as Mexican American, another
as Latina, and the last as Puerto Rican. Interestingly, the teacher who self-
identified as Latina (i.e., Lucero) later indicated that this categorization mani-
fested when she moved to the United States, when she felt compelled to specify
a category of race (i.e., whereas in Venezuela, she expressed that most people
identified as Venezuelan, regardless of skin tone, which she also problematized).

At the time of the study, all three of the collaborators were Spanish teachers who worked at high schools with a predominantly Black student population. More specifically, as of 2021, in Consuelo's school 86 % of students were
Black, 11 % were White, and 3 % were Latinx; in Lucero's school 86 % of
students were Black, 10 % were Latinx, 3 % were White, and 1 % were two or
more races; and in Mercedes' school 60 % of students were Black, 23 % were
White, 14 % were Latinx, 2 % were Asian, and 1 % were two or more races
(National Center for Education Statistics, n.d.). Lucero and Mercedes worked
at schools with a significant number of Latinx students, based on the relatively
small but increasing amount of Latinx students in the Greater Birmingham
Metropolitan Area.

During the 2020–2021 academic year in which the study took place, the
global COVID-19 pandemic provoked many unforeseen, unavoidable, and
unique circumstances under which the three Latina teachers were working
and teaching in their respective school districts. Of the three Latina teachers,
two worked in the same school district (i.e., Consuelo and Mercedes) whose
school year was delayed by the pandemic. Once the school year commenced,
students attended school virtually until mid-October though many students
remained virtual. Mercedes gained permission to teach virtually due to underlying health concerns, thus her students that returned to in-person instruction
attended class with a substitute teacher with Mercedes providing instruction
remotely. Lucero's school year began virtually and though students got permission to return to in-person instruction, many of her students remained virtual.
Both school districts in which the teachers worked did not require students
to turn on their video cameras during virtual instruction. In fact, in Consuelo and Mercedes' school district, students were not required to turn on their
microphones, due to concerns about potentially liable background noises. All
three Latina teachers expressed stress and frustration with their teaching situ-
ations during the first year of COVID-19.

**Table 1:** *Latina Teacher Participants/Collaborators*

| Name | Cultural Identity | Age | Birthplace | Marital/Partner Status | Dependents | Years in AL | Years of Teaching Experience | Content Area | Students of Color at School (NCES, n.d.) |
|---|---|---|---|---|---|---|---|---|---|
| Consuelo | Mexican American | 55 | Texas | Married | 2 | 20 | 19 | Spanish | 86 % Black 3 % Latinx |
| Lucero | Latina | 57 | Venezuela | Widow | 0 | 18 | 25 | Spanish | 86 % Black 10 % Latinx |
| Mercedes | Puerto Rican | 39 | Puerto Rico | Single | 0 | 16 | 13 | Spanish | 60 % Black 14 % Latinx 2.2 % Asian |

# Collecting the Data

Data collection for the original study upon which this book is based occurred via a pre- and post informational questionnaire, three individual in-depth interviews, three book pláticas, an altered book/artistic artifact, and ethnographic field notes. Table two provides a brief synopsis of the data collection methods. The following sub-sections are divided by the type of data collection with details and information about each method.

**Table 2:** *Data Collection Summary*

| Type of Collection | Description of Collection | Purpose of Collection |
|---|---|---|
| Informational Questionnaire | Pre- and post ten-item questionnaire completed at the beginning of the first and second individual interview sessions | Informal means to capture personal and reflective information in the Latina teachers' own words |
| Individual In-Depth Interviews/Conversations | Three interviews – the first occurring before the first book *plática*, the second occurring after the last book *plática*, and the third happening at the end of the study for member checking | Intimate means to build rapport with each Latina teacher and gather individual information relative to their personal, familial, and schooling histories; means to solicit feedback and revisions via member checking |
| Book *Plática* Focus Group Questions and Discussion | Three book gatherings occurring three tofour weeks after each young adult book was read, where focus group questions and discussion occured | Communal means to *platicar* and share reactions and experiences similar to and different from those depicted in the young adult books |
| Altered Book Artifacts | Individual vintage books used as an art journal during each of the three book *pláticas* | Reflective means to respond to young adult literature, book characters, and Latina teachers' experiences |
| Ethnographic Field Notes | Ongoing notes capturing sensory details, quotes, descriptions, and observations taken throughout the study, both during and after interviews and *pláticas* | Sensory and observational means to gather details about the collaborators to include in the testimonios |

## Questionnaires

The pre- and post questionnaires for the original study occurred at the beginning of the first and second individual in-depth interview conversations. Each questionnaire contained eleven questions and lasted 10–15-minutes to complete. The pre-questionnaire included six short-answer response questions ranging from general inquiries like "name" and "age," to personal questions regarding cultural identification and language(s) spoken (see Appendix B). It also included five questions with rating scales including numbers one-ten (e.g., "interested," "somewhat interested," or "not interested"; "very comfortable," "somewhat comfortable," or "not comfortable"). The post-questionnaire included two of the same short-answer personal information questions from the pre-questionnaire, the same five questions with rating scales from the pre-questionnaire, and three additional short-answer questions relative to the Latina teachers' experiences in the study (e.g., what they gained from the study and what they would change about the study [see Appendix B]).

## Interviews

The three individual in-depth interviews/conversations for this study were audio-recorded and lasted approximately 90–120 minutes (see Appendix C). The purpose of the first interview was to complete the pre-questionnaire and gather information relative to each teacher's personal and schooling experiences, including teaching experiences. The purpose of the second interview was to ask followup questions and complete the post-questionnaire. The third interview was intended to share initial findings and emerging themes and enact member checking by having each teacher review and provide feedback on descriptions and quotes.

## *Book Pláctica*

Each book plática began with a series of focus group questions (See Appendix D) and subsequent discussion based on the collaborators' reactions to the main characters, themes, and events in each YAL book (see Appendix A). The pláticas acted as fluid conversations between the teachers, allowing us to build trust through mutual sharing and vulnerability (Espino et al., 2010; Flores & García, 2009; Fierros & Delgado Bernal, 2016).

Table 2

While this study did not explore literary theories and did not seek to expound upon literary scholarship as related to Latinx texts, it relied upon the perspectives of both Cai (2002) and Garcia (2017) to use Latinx YAL books to critically explore the lives of female Latina characters as a means to reflect on the teachers' own narratives, experiences, and notions of Latinidad. The stories about these Latina characters involved their lived experiences as, for example, first generation immigrants, second generation immigrants, urban life experiences, language diversity, colorism, imposter syndrome, and body image . . . all of which included a focus on how aspects of identity intersect at multiple levels, to include how their gendered and Latina hybridity impacted their lives.

Every *plática* included ten short-answer-response questions about the teachers' reactions and opinions about the main characters, themes, and events in the young adult books. For example, questions regarding with which character the teachers most related, personal memories that were evoked by the book, and how the teachers related to the challenges of assimilation presented in each book were explored. Thus, by examining the book characters, the Latina teachers and I disrupted conventional narratives about what it meant to be authentic Latinas by including opportunities to explore their geography of self during the book *pláticas*. The multiplicity of Latina identities present in each young adult book were explored, in addition to a discussion about the intersectionalities of the Latina characters' lives. Each *plática* also included an altered book reflective task that the teachers individually completed.

Questions for the book *pláticas* were used as "a collaborative process comprised of sharing stories, building community, and acknowledging multiple realities and vulnerabilities" (Burciaga & Tavares, 2006, p. 805). Thus, the teachers were viewed with *respeto*/respect and as individuals with valuable knowledge, as "contributors and co-constructors of the meaning making process," since the experiences, narratives, and perspectives that they shared comprised the content from which meaning was created in the study (Fierros & Delgado Bernal, 2016, p. 111). More specifically, the teachers were not simply ethnographic informants, but were collaborators whose personal interactions with each other during the *pláticas* acted as a means to establish meaningful connection and intimate opportunities to co-construct knowledge based on their lived experiences (Fierros & Delgado Bernal, 2016; Godinez, 2006). The conversational format of *pláticas* offered a fluid dialogue between the teacher contributors, allowing us to engage in two-way conversation built on establishing trust through mutual sharing and vulnerability (Espino et al., 2010; Flores

& Garcia, 2009; Fierros & Delgado Bernal, 2016). Thus, the book plática questions provided a map of themes to guide the plática and were not used as rigid scripts. The book pláticas provided an opportunity for the teachers to explore who they were and who they were becoming on a continual basis via the YAL texts, altered book reflections, and collaborations with each other – all of these data collection points paved a path for them to make meaning together.

## Altered Books

The altered books were reflective artifacts that the teachers used to respond to prompts (See Appendix E) aimed at extending their thinking and generating deeper self-reflections about the multicultural YAL (i.e., similar to a visual journal with drawings and collages). The altered books were completed during the book pláticas in order to facilitate conversation, build community, and respond to the book plática questions. The altered books also initiated points

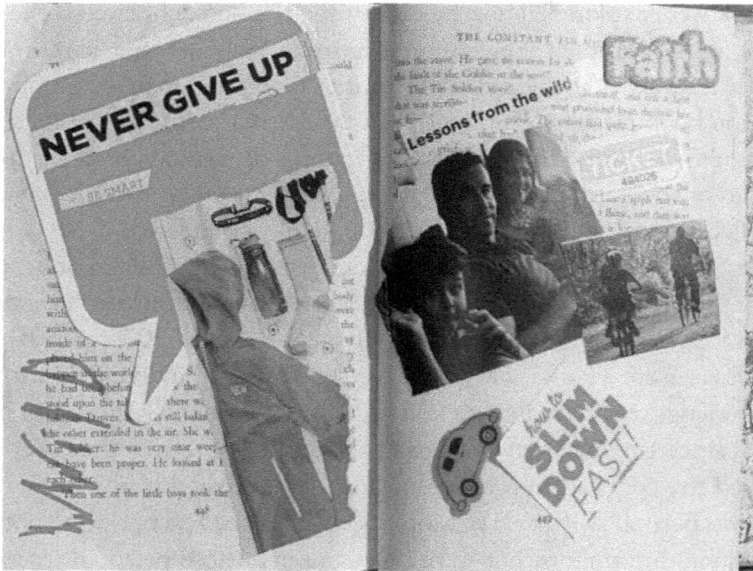

Figure 2: *Sample of Altered Book Task One*
Note. Visual depiction of Latina teacher (Consuelo) on the inside and outside. Left side depicts Consuelo's outside – the quote bubble represented her outspoken nature; she encourages others, enjoys the outdoors, and is adventurous. Right side depicts Consuelo's inside – ticket and car represent her desire to get away; she's family oriented, quick-paced, and spiritual.

of discussion during the book pláticas, in addition to provoking clarifying and probing followup interview questions for the third/final interview conversation with the teachers.

Each altered book task was intended to be completed by visually depicting the YAL character reflection on one side of the book and the Latina teachers' reflection on the other side of the book, so that the two-page layout spread depicted a visual comparison between the YAL character and the Latina teacher. Each task concluded with the same reflective questions – namely, asking the Latina teacher what advice she would give the main YAL character, a reflection of the day's task, and an artist's statement about the meaning behind the final product for the day's plática.

These altered books served as "aesthetic strategies for resisting dominant cultural norms" (Anzaldúa, 1990, p. xxiv) and as an alternative way for participants to critically engage with the multicultural young adult literature in a non-normative manner (i.e., by resisting traditional forms of knowledge-making and research gathering). In other words, rather than solely implement traditional modes of research data collection like surveys, the altered

Figure 3: *Sample of Altered Book Task Two*
Note. Visual depiction of protagonist's wants and resulting conflicts. Ballerina represents protagonist's balancing of challenges; how she wants to escape and learn more about her mother's faith; and how she remembers her sister (two hearts).

Figure 4: *Sample of Altered Book Task Three*
Note. Visual depiction of one of the Latina teacher's (Mercedes) superpowers. Her students, her Puerto Rican identity, her Latina roots, her family, and her educator status in Alabama are her self-identified superpowers.

books served as a humanizing methodology aimed at generating self-reflection and self-awareness by way of artistic expression (i.e., the altered books humanized the Latina teachers' lived experiences). "An aesthetic experience can be described as the relationship created between an observer and a specific artwork, and the way that work of art affects the observer in light of his/her background and personal history," (Medina, 2009, p. 59) thus, the altered books engaged the Latina teachers in an immersive and layered aesthetic experience – first by engaging with young adult literature (one form of art) and then by creating altered books based on the relationship developed by interacting with the young adult literature.

## Ethnographic Field Notes

Ethnographic field notes, both reflective and descriptive, were written throughout the study. Prior to every interview conversation and plática,

I reminded the teachers about why I was taking occasional notes during our interactions – I was careful to inform them that the field notes aided in providing details for the testimonios, in addition to helping me get to know them better. Informing the teachers of my intentions and actions about treading with sensitivity and respeto was essential, so that they felt seen and heard (i.e., versus being ignored as I took quick notes). I also drew on my own experiences and cultural intuition (Monzó, 2015) to help guide descriptions and jottings.

My field notes conveyed initial impressions, significant and unexpected occurrences, and descriptions of the teachers and how they interacted with each other. Additionally, "jottings" were used to record "key words and phrases" that were later used "to construct evocative descriptions of the scene" (Emerson, Fretz, & Shaw, 2011, p. 29). Thus, jottings included sensory details, quotes, and feelings (i.e., including my own and the collaborators' feelings), in addition to being careful not to generalize (Emerson et al., 2011). Furthermore, the jottings and field notes included "interim texts" (Clandinin & Connelly, 2000) and restorying that conveyed descriptions of the aforementioned via different genres, points of view (e.g., first person, past tense, etc.), and for different purposes (i.e., including drafts of testimonios).

In the midst of writing field notes, I also wrote what Johnny Saldaña (2016) describes as analytic memos that focused on: reflecting upon emerging themes, posing questions, exploring how I personally related to the emerging themes and field note reflections, describing how the theoretical frameworks were intersecting with emerging patterns, examining problems with the study, identifying future areas of research, and answering some of the research/inquiry questions. Throughout the reflective process of writing analytic memos, I employed criticality that was centered on my own deeply personal and cultural experiences as a Latina navigating predominantly non-Latinx spaces in the Deep South. Thus, I continued to rely heavily on my cultural intuition (Calderon, Delgado Bernal, Velez, Perez Huber, & Malagon, 2012; Delgado Bernal, 1998, 2012; Monzó, 2015).

## Information About YAL Texts Used in the Book Pláticas

The three young adult books that were read for the book pláticas were *Knitting the Fog* by Claudia D. Hernandez (2019), *I am Not Your Perfect Mexican*

*Daughter* by Erika L. Sanchez (2017), and *The Poet* X by Elizabeth Acevedo (2019 [see Appendix A]). The three texts were selected based on the following criteria: contemporary YAL written within the past five-ten years; critical fiction aimed at addressing culture and *Latinidad* as fluid and complex; a Latina adolescent as the main character; characters with intersecting identities; themes about family and mother/daughter relationships; use of English and/or Spanish language explicitly addressed in the story's narrative ark; varying insider and outsider cultural perspectives; stories about Latina adolescents from three different Latinx perspectives; Latina authors (Alamillo, 2007). The YAL texts emphasized main characters as agents of change and problematized the notion that being Latina (or Latinidad in general) is not a sole monolithic entity – the YAL cultivated variations in the characters' stories and experiences, even within one family (e.g., the sisters in *I'm Not Your Perfect Mexican Daughter* [Sanchez, 2017]).

*Knitting the Fog* (Hernandez, 2019) tells the story of Claudia, who lives in Guatemala with her family until her mother flees to the United States to get away from her abusive father when she's seven years old. Claudia and her two older sisters are temporarily raised by their great aunt and grandmother until they move to Los Angeles to join their mother when Claudia is ten years old. Upon moving to a predominantly Mexican neighborhood, Claudia faces challenges assimilating, learning English, and balancing the parts of herself that make her unique.

*I am Not Your Perfect Mexican Daughter* (Sanchez, 2017) tells the story of Julia, who struggles to fulfill her parents' expectations of a Mexican daughter after her older sister tragically dies. Throughout the novel, Julia attempts to balance managing her family's grief (in particular, her mother) and learning secrets about her sister, all of which lead to emotional instability that culminate in Julia being sent to visit her family in Mexico. Ultimately, Julia explores her identity and learns about family secrets that help her better understand her mother.

*The Poet* X (Acevedo, 2019) is about Xiomara, who is from the Dominican Republic and lives in Harlem. She doesn't fit the traditional role of a feminine Latina daughter and struggles to be understood by her parents, especially her mother. Written in verse/poems, Xiomara explores her feelings of cultural isolation and resilient strength via her poetry slam poems. Table two depicts a summary of the YAL texts, themes, issues that were problematized, main conflicts and resolutions, and the goals for using the texts.

**Table 3:** *Synopsis of YAL Texts Used*

| YAL Title | Protagonist's Cultural Ethnicity | Main Conflict | Main Resolution | Major Theme(s) | Problematized Issues | Goals for Text Usage |
|---|---|---|---|---|---|---|
| *Knitting the Fog* | Guatemalan | Undocumented journey and acclimation into U.S. | Cultural education leads to self-acceptance | Acceptance of hybrid identity | English fluency and accents | Intergenerational, intercultural, and intracultural threads |
| *I'm Not Your Perfect Mexican Daughter* | Mexican | Rejection by family for bicultural identity | Family history as means to understanding self | Secrets and denial of cultural history | Latinx mother/daughter relationships | Privileges Latinx cultural ways of being |
| *The Poet X* | Dominican Republic | Rejection of gendered roles and resulting tensions | Writing as a vehicle of change and understanding self | Cultural isolation and resiliency | Gendered Latinx roles | Privileges alternative Latinx ways of knowing |

# Analyzing the Data

LatCrit and Chicana/Latina Feminism were the lenses I used in interpreting emerging themes and translating the collaborators' narratives by way of "restorying" (Creswell & Poth, 2018). Emotion coding was used to identify emotions that surfaced by the participants and/or myself, while values coding was used to identify "values, attitudes, and beliefs, representing [the collaborators'] perspectives or worldview" (Saldaña, 2016, p. 131). The development of "interim texts," written at different times, for different purposes, and in different genres also occurred during the entire data analysis and data collection phases (Clandinin & Connelly, 2000).

Like Delgado Bernal (1998), I relied on my cultural intuition in several ways in the study. For example, I relied on my cultural intuition to advocate for empathy and understanding about and among the different teachers who represented varying Latinx countries and cultures, including my own Puerto Rican ethnicity. Given the complicated and tension/trauma-filled history that exists among different Latinx groups, to include citizenship status, Indigenous roots, and Afrocentricity, I imbued intracultural Latinx empathy by explaining my intentions of creating a space where the Latinx teachers could discuss their experiences inside or outside of the young adult literature that was used in the study. I also relied on my cultural intuition by sharing my own ancestral stories, when appropriate. I extended Delgado Bernal's (1998) notion of Chicana Feminist epistemology by including varying and multiple Latina identities, and purposefully using the term Chicana/Latina Feminism to encompass Chicana Feminist epistemology in education that extends to the multiplicity of Latinas.[1]

These individual and collective stories resulted in testimonios grounded in an epistemology of Chicana/Latina Feminism. Elements of portraiture strongly guided the development of the testimonios, in that I actively selected themes and patterns "to tell the story [-] strategic in deciding on points of focus and emphasis, and creative in defining the sequence and rhythm of the narrative" (Lawrence-Lightfoot, 2005, p. 10). Thus, my ethnographic perspective and voice is present in the testimonios, just as "the self of the portraitist emerges as an instrument of inquiry, an eye on perspective taking, an ear that discerns nuances, and a voice that speaks and offers insights" (Lawrence-Lightfoot, 2005, p. 11). The testimonios featured in this book have been imbued with "Muxerista Portraiture," which partners Chicana Feminist Theory with portraiture to incorporate the unique experiences of Chicanas (Flores, 2017a, 2017b). I did, however, focus on the broader category of Latinas, not solely Chicanas.

# My Positionality

As a Puerto Rican educator who formerly worked as an English Language Arts teacher in Miami, Florida, I have been committed to enriching the schooling experiences of Latinx students. Residing in Alabama for 15 years, I was immediately intrigued about the ways in which culture intersects with the schooling environment for Latinx students and teachers. Given my own struggles with simultaneously seeking, yet rejecting affirmations of successful assimilation, I became deeply interested in the ways in which Latina teachers navigate their cultural experiences in spaces where they represent a vast minority (i.e., in predominantly White or Black spaces). The fact that I can pass as and present as White and am often denied my Latina existence has deepened my desire for authentic connection with other Latinas. It is for these reasons that I aimed to explore the lived experiences of Latina teachers by uniquely positioning my own experiences with that of a participant observer. Indeed, every part of the study was aimed at building trust, developing reciprocity between and among the collaborators (including me), sharing vulnerability, and promoting healing and love. These aims, however, were not absent of my own biases. I had to frequently allow myself to truly listen to the teachers and their various expressions, versus relying on my own expectations and assumptions about them and their experiences (e.g., how they navigated within their academic and interpersonal environments). I had to consistently trust the process of learning from the knowledge they were sharing, and I had to commit to authentically describing their multifaceted portraitures in a way that would honor their complex and beautiful essences. Ultimately, much like the collages that the collaborators created in their altered books, the theoretical framework, methodological approach and strategies, data collection, and data analysis mirrored the process and product of a collage of Latina teacher narratives grounded in healing, love, and empowerment resulting from the strength of such counter-narratives (i.e., to include the Latina characters in the YAL).

# Conclusion

All of the data collection methods and strong Chicana/Latina Feminist methodological approaches, such as pláticas, YAL texts written by Latinas, visual data representations of self via altered books, and the testimonios with aspects of portraiture, were aimed to "confront the research process with our[/Latina] total selves – our grief, our fears, our desires, and our love" (Calderon et al.,

2012, p. 534). LatCrit and Chicana/Latina Feminism facilitated learning about and sharing life experiences in relation to a shared cultural community and an individual within that community (i.e., via a narrative ethnographic approach). These frameworks provided a deeper understanding of how Latina teachers explicated their sense of belonging as they sought to practice and better define their cultural identities. These frameworks also allowed for researcher subjectivity, since they encouraged me, the researcher, to rely on my own cultural intuition and experiential knowledge to investigate the Latina collaborators' lived experiences (thereby validating the knowledge and meaning we produced as Latinas).

The following chapter centers the individual testimonios that are based on the stories and narratives shared by the Latina teacher participants via individual interviews, the whole-group book pláticas, and the altered books that each teacher created based on their connections to the young adult literature that was read. Testimonios were used as empowering and transformative forms of narrative that aimed to produce an intensified collective consciousness among the Latina educators, without essentializing Latina teachers as a whole (Anzaldua, 1987; Espino et al., 2010; Godinez, 2006; The Latina Feminist Group, 2001).

# Note

1 In full transparency and humility, I have struggled to approach and convey how seminal and contemporary literature about Chicana feminism and Chicana feminist epistemology in education does not explicitly describe or advocate for a Latina feminism that is inclusive of all Latinas; or how such a Latina feminism could aim to evoke unity and solidarity among Latinas (i.e., particularly given the current sociopolitical forces that instigate divisiveness among diverse groups, including Latinxs).

# · 3 ·

# CUENTOS Y TESTIMONIOS

This book and the narrative ethnographic study upon which it is based, includes multiple frameworks aimed at cultivating an exploration of the lived experiences of three Latina teacher collaborators in the Deep South. From the LatCrit and Chicana/Latina Feminist frameworks to the testimonios with muxerista portraiture, these frameworks and methods acted as trenzas aimed at weaving the multilayered complexities and uniquities that comprised the lives of the three Latina teachers. The book pláticas highlighted how fostering and holding space together yielded three broad themes about family, belongingness, and empowerment that were evident in the stories the teachers recounted. Moreover, the pláticas sought to create a space of support and encouragement, where the Latina teachers felt comfortable to express their trenzas, which represented their hybrid and multifaceted identities. This book plática space (Gutierrez, Baquedano-Lopez, & Tejada, 1999; García & Gaddes, 2012) was reinforced via the use of three young adult literature (YAL) texts and the teachers' mixed use of languages (e.g., using Spanish and/or English). Additionally, this space was an area where the collaborators relied on their own narratives and counter-narratives to critically examine their lives in relation to the YAL characters and themselves (i.e., Latinas representing different Latinidades).

To respetar/respect and interweave the narrative threads and themes surrounding the thoughtful and at times painful stories the teacher collaborators shared, this chapter is devoted to individual testimonios imbued with muxerista portraiture for each Latina teacher. The muxerista portraiture allows for reliance on the lived experiences of Latinas "to paint portraits committed to social justice and challenging all forms of subordination" (Flores, 2017a). The voice I used to construct the testimonios imbued with muxerista portraiture is more audible and reflective, highlighting "my purpose in telling two intertwined stories:" one that traces the teacher's lived experiences and the other that reflects my developing relationship with them and their experiences (Lawrence-Lightfoot & Davis, 1997, p. 259). Thus, as Goodall (2000) stressed, the testimonios are "self-reflexive" and:

> [They are] told through the voice of a narrator who isn't shy about examining her- or himself as she or he examines others and contexts. Self-reflexive moments are used to add personal background information to an account, reveal the author's complicity in how something happened, or pose difficult questions that do not necessarily have clearly defined answers. (p. 196)

Within the testimonios, muxerista portraiture merges Chicana/Latina Feminism with Lawrence-Lightfoot's concept of portraiture by focusing on "convergent threads" and dissonant threads and "illuminating metaphors" (Lawrence-Lightfoot & Davis, 1997, p. 185) that are guided by my cultural intuition as a Latina with a "Chicana/Latina feminist sensibility" (Flores, 2017a, p. 2). The first thread of each testimonio begins with a found poem, which I created by solely using the collaborators' words and direct quotes that they shared during individual conversations, book pláticas, altered books, and/ or questionnaires. I made the decision to use their own words so their language could be experienced and read in a loving way that celebrates their uniqueness, genialidad/genius, beauty, and love. The first thread is the found poems, followed by the testimonios, and culminating in a description of themes.

## Consuelo's Testimonio

Stay true to yourself.
You don't have to be just who they say you are.

You can only be you.

I'm just the invisible one –
because here,

you're either Black or you're White,
there's nothing in between.

You never think of yourself
as being less than anybody else.

Stay true to yourself.

We talk with our hands a lot.
But somewhere along the way somebody saidsomething
and I had to sit on my hands
so that I wouldn't use them too much.

At school and work, even though I may have the answer to something,
I'm not the one they go to.

You don't have to be just who they say you are.

You want to say things,
but you can't say them
because they're not the right thing to say.

I don't think I've ever
been an insider.

You can only be you.

As a Spanish teacher,
it's like I want to
get rid of all those stereotypes.

This is why you go to school.
You have to wait until [awareness] opens for you.

Stay true to yourself.
You don't have to be just who they say you are.
You can only be you.

You can only be you.

When I first met Consuelo, she was already waiting for me, sitting at a wooden picnic table at the public park we had agreed upon. The worn-in pine wood of the table sat under a large cedar gazebo. I was rushing from my last interview, and it had just started to sprinkle rain. It was still summer, and school was about to begin in a way that no one could have ever predicted. We were already about five months into the COVID-19 pandemic, and no one had fully realized just how drastically the beginning of the academic year would prove to be, especially Consuelo.

We sat socially distanced on opposite ends of the table, both wearing cloth masks. I pushed my smartphone close to Consuelo and began recording.

Consuelo appeared curious yet cautious. Her responses were efficient and direct, which is to say . . . to the point. Upon learning that she had served in the Army for eight years and was raised among multiple military family members (to include her father), her directness made sense. Given my own background as an Army-Brat with a father and two grandfathers who had served in the Army and made it their career, I understood her desire for succinctness. I was almost relieved that our interview, the last one I had scheduled for the day, was going so expeditiously.

From the beginning, it was clear how Consuelo's Mexican-American family in Texas represented her Home.[1] She described Home as Texas, even though she had resided in Alabama for 20 years. Consuelo came across as an adventurous spirit that, like many of us, had become anchored to a place that was somewhat foreign to her roots. She had resided in Alabama yet yearned to get away – "sometimes I just want to get into my little car and just keep going somewhere." Home is where she goes and has gone every summer. She described how on the last day of school every year her car is packed and ready to go. On the last day of school, she begins her journey from Alabama to Texas. When her children were younger, they would accompany her, but now she travels alone – Consuelo laughed as she proclaimed that this was the secret to her marriage . . . spending an entire summer with her family in Texas, away from her husband, but among her parents, aunts, uncles, great aunts, great uncles, and a slew of cousins. Home is mixing Spanish and English and seamlessly traveling between the Texas and Mexico border.

Consuelo frequently referenced the plight and symbolic resonance of the strong mujeres in her family. She noted that "the women are very strong in my family because they have to be." She was raised by the women in her family who always said, "'You do better if you want to do better. But it's on you if you want to do more." Consuelo recounted how her grandmother would take her siblings and cousins to work, where she cleaned houses and would say, "See, this is why you don't do this. This is why you go to school, so you don't have to sit here and look at this again." She recounted how her mother insisted that she go to college first before joining the Army – "She said, 'Once you give me that piece of paper with your name on it, then you can go do whatever.'"

It is from her family that Consuelo attributed her sense of service, kindness, follow-through, loyalty, commitment, diligence, compassion, and inner strength. During the final book plática, upon discussing the main character of *Knitting the Fog* (Hernandez, 2019) and the poverty she experienced in Guatemala, Consuelo shared how her family did what they had to do to get by when her father, deployed and away from Texas, didn't send sufficient money. She recalled being in the third grade and being sent out to sell tamales that her mother had made. Later, during our second conversation, Consuelo stressed how she was raised to give help whenever someone asked for it – "my parents were like that, my grandmother was like that, so I guess it's just part of who we are as a family. If people ask for help, you give it." She also reflected on the importance of always teaching, especially with her own kids –

It's all about teaching, wanting them to be better. I know in our family it has been from way down, you want them [your kids] to be better than you were, because that's the job. That's what you're supposed to do, make them better than you. Not necessarily have things better than you, just be better.

As I listened to Consuelo, it became increasingly clear that she felt overlooked and diminished. She expressed feeling both ignored and overused –

"Ah, we'll get her. She's a doormat, you can do whatever. She'll do it." At school and work, even though I may have the answer to something, I'm not the one they go to – either because they think I don't know how . . . and then when I do say I know, they're like, really surprised like, "really?" Even here within my husband's family it's the same way too with some of his family.

While these conclusions applied to her school/teaching environment, I was hesitant to probe too much about her personal and family life. Consuelo readily confirmed that she was guarded and protective about her innermost feelings and experiences, yet it was evident that by the end of the study, Consuelo was the collaborator who had traversed the longest introspective journey that landed her within Anzaldúa's in-between or "liminal spaces" of nepantla (Anzaldúa, 2015, p. 74). She commented sentiments like, "You want to say things, but you can't say them because they're not the right thing to say." and "Until somebody shows you, you don't know you're not seeing things. Until somebody tells you, you don't know." Later, during one of our last conversations, she affirmed, "This [experience] has really been an eye opener. It's kind of sad that I just now, at this age, am just realizing it. You just kind of go along and not even think about it." At the last book plática she emphasized, "The word that I pulled out was changing, coming back to the roots, because I never really used to think about who I really was, I was just me."

By our final conversation Consuelo's sense of isolation and stress was palpable. It had been about two weeks since our final book plática, where she had mentioned how much she enjoyed meeting in-person to chat and craft with the altered books tasks. She described how she remained in her classroom planning and organizing until well after 4pm every day. She was struggling to remain optimistic given her school's updated requirement of submitting lesson plans two-four weeks in advance of implementing instruction. She expressed how tired she was:

> I'm so tired. I'm just tired. I can't teach the way I want to teach the way things are going right now [with virtual and remote learning]. I can't see the kids. I like to get up and move, and they're like, "What are you doing?" The screen only picks up so much, you just can't move the way you want to.

She was tired and yet she remained hopeful for and about her students. She was forgiving of her students' biases and expressed how she patiently explained things to her students like, "Y'all don't understand. My family does not want to come here. They're doctors, they're nurses, they're pharmacists. They don't want to come here and be gardeners because nobody else wants to give them their same job that they're equal to." She has enjoyed and thrives off of being able to dispel negative stereotypes about Latinxs, in addition to being hopeful about what she teaches regarding cultural nuances and how such nuances will make a difference in the lives of her students – "I put a lot of FYIs out there about things, just to let them know that there's more out there – and not to be so close-minded." Consuelo's sense of awareness and criticality has begun to awaken, as evidenced from the following:

> I'm staying away from the sugar skulls [and not just showing commercialized sugar skulls to teach El Dia de Los Muertos/Day of the Dead], I'm staying away from, you know, all the little colorful things and really focusing on what is the meaning of it; why is that so important to remember who you are and where you came from. Because even here in the States, people don't ever think about who they are or where they came from, they just are. And I picked up a lot of that too. So, now, it's like I'm changing, trying to go back and say, "I get who I am" because of this, this, and this. And you really, now that I think about it, you really can't move forward without knowing who you are. That's what I tell my students – how do you know what you're going to do if you don't know who you are, who you're becoming?

## Lucero's Testimonio

I just don't want to label.

Or you are Black, White, or Mexican,

but I am not
    Black
    White or
    Mexican,
so, where do I fit in?

If you don't fit,
you don't feel welcome anywhere.

I just want to be,
this is Lucero the human being,
with no labels.

I just don't want to label.

Your la nd is inserted in your soul.

I have learned from other cultures
and I have learned respect
and understanding from other cultures.

If you know the population, you are teaching
and understand their culture –
you will understand what kind of
teacher you should be.

Nunca dejes de ser tu misma,
no le des importancia al acento –
el acento te hace unica.[2]

Your land is inserted in your soul.

It was a warm August day when I parked in front of Lucero's house and walked up the steps to her concrete porch. She had been looking out for my arrival and quickly opened her wooden front door to greet me. Her dark hair was loosely tied back, with eyeglasses framing her darkened and richly bronzed skin. She wore a long bohemian skirt and knit top that snuggly hugged her torso. This interview would mark my very first in-depth individual conversation for the study. I had assumed and was slightly anxious that our conversation might be conducted solely in Spanish, since maneuvering Spanish with individuals from different Latinx countries can make me feel self-conscious about my own Latina authenticity and ability to speak Spanish "correctly" or fluently. Puerto Ricans have often been stigmatized for speaking Spanish "incorrectly," for not pronouncing their "r's" and "l's," and thus speaking an inferior type of Spanish. Anzaldúa reminds me that like Chicanos, Puerto Ricans like me have "internalized the belief that we speak poor Spanish . . . [a]nd because we internalize how our language has been used against us by the dominant culture, we use our language differences against each other" (2007, p. 80). Thus, I was secretly and ashamedly relieved that Lucero rarely spoke Spanish to me during our interview, thus lessening my insecurities of authenticity. Speaking in English would remain the norm, except during some of the book pláticas, where she occasionally interspersed her speech with Spanish. I'd like to think that this was due to our increasing sense of community, connection, and confianza/trust, though I never outright asked any of the collaborators under what circumstances they chose to speak Spanish in informal settings. I remained curious, however, about what made individuals like Lucero, who donned heavy English accents that revealed their Latinx background, from automatically relying on Spanish when speaking to Spanish speakers. It wasn't until Lucero gave advice to one of the YAL text characters that I realized how much I had to learn from her – I remembered her writing, "Toma las cosas con calma, la fluidez del lenguaje llega con el tiempo y la practica. Nunca dejes de ser tu misma, no le des importancia al acento; el acento te hace unica." (Take things with calm, the fluency of language will come with time and practice. Never stop being who you are, don't give importance to your accent ... that accent is what makes you unique.).

During our first conversation, Lucero's free-spirited nature was immediately apparent as was her sense of curiosity and openness to learning from and about others. She described how her nature of acceptance toward others was based on her Bahai faith, which is "based on looking for the oneness of humankind – understanding and loving the differences of everybody regardless of race, regardless of identity, cultural identity, regardless of even religious background." I remember being intrigued about her personal life when she began describing that when she was younger, she had wanted to be an airplane mechanic, but was quickly told girls didn't become mechanics. She then expressed what became a life-long interest in and passion for music – she taught herself to play the guitar when she was 10 years old and became the sole female in her family to play an instrument. After pursuing medical school and realizing hospitals weren't an environment she wanted to be surrounded by, she finished her degree in biology and biology education.

Teaching Spanish was a profession that Lucero had come to in a more practical manner. She had taught biology in Venezuela for eight years and upon moving to Alabama 19 years ago she taught biology and some Spanish courses at a private school. She quickly became disillusioned when parents complained about why she was showing parts of *An Inconvenient Truth*

(Guggenheim, 2006) – "I don't want to teach science in this country, it's too complicated." She recalled an interaction with her headmaster at the school in which she began teaching in the U.S. as follows:

> "Ms. Lucero, parents are calling and complaining about why you are showing an Al Gore movie." I had no knowledge about why they were asking me this because I had no [political] knowledge ... I don't even follow politics. Al Gore? And I said, "Well, this is a documentary, and I was showing pieces of the documentary explaining causes and consequences of global warming that have to do with the curriculum that is required by the state of Alabama."

And so, she continued teaching, but chose to solely teach Spanish. It was teaching Spanish, however, that she genuinely came to love. The ability to teach Latinx cultures ultimately brought her joy and passion. Lucero joyfully shared how she could rely on her own experiences, in addition to relating her experiences to other Latinx cultures and the cultural experiences of her students. Her hands and facial expressions became enlivened as she described how she introduced different Latinx music, customs, expressions, and foods into her curriculum.

Lucero's independent and steadfast nature allowed her to almost repel any sentiments aimed at diminishing her inner fire. During our second conversation, she shared how she was hired to teach Spanish in a wealthier school district, but her teaching contract had not been renewed after one year. She indicated that the reason for her non-renewal hadn't occurred to her until other people pointed it out –

> I was new in the country and I still didn't know ... they were supposed to give me up to three years to work on my certification, they didn't do it for me. They did it for other people, they didn't do it for me. And there are reasons for it. They don't explicitly tell you, but I don't think I had the right color, not the right accent. But you know, I didn't consider that that was the case until other people told me, You know that it wasn't the certification Ms. Lucero, it was [the district]."

Lucero's sense of self-acceptance was very likely tied to how grounded and accepted by her family she felt. She recalled how her family frequently sat together to eat dinner, her father asking questions and telling jokes. She remembered how much her mother loved to read, reading anything from magazines to her favorite bible. In fact, it was her mother who held especially high educational aspirations for her and her seven siblings. Her childhood home was filled with singing and music, chores, and autonomy. It was also a place where education was valued and expected – "My parents, as long as I was engaged in education, studying something, they didn't care. 'That's what makes you happy? This is what you want to do? Go for it! You want to do that? Go for it!'" So long as her and her siblings earned a college education, her parents supported any desired career path.

Lucero described herself as being introverted, inspired by creativity and curiosity, and deeply loyal to and protective of the people she loves. During the book pláticas she tended to listen more intently than share her own opinions, but she was always present and engaged with the altered book tasks. It was pleasantly surprising, therefore, when she described her sentiments about her Home (i.e., Venezuela) and the immigrant experiences in the YAL texts. She expressed the following:

> ... there are no borders, but you still have to cross a border ... your land is inserted in your soul. If you're not an immigrant, you cannot understand. You leave part of your soul in your own country. The people who come here from Central America and Mexico, they are coming escaping a situation that they had to, and they don't come because they want to, it's because they have to. It's a difference, it's a different feeling.

Lucero was keenly aware of the immigrant's plight to America, particularly since she has been the only person in her family to live in the United States. She came to Alabama by way of marrying a White man from Birmingham who practiced the same Bahai faith yet passed away two years ago. In fact, during our first conversation, Lucero mentioned that she had benefitted from her White husband's privilege and had initially felt scared and unprotected when he died, and she no longer had "White protection." She continued to live in the same home she shared with her husband and expressed that her neighbors treated her "just like a neighbor" and not "as negatively 'Hispanic'."

Lucero was especially sensitive to and grateful for the Latinx experiences depicted in the YAL texts –

> The books raise awareness of what the Latino community is going through in this process of trying to fit in and the process of why they are here; the struggles with the language and the cultural shock. There is the issue of adapting to or accepting a new culture and trying to incorporate that culture into your life, because you want to fit in with the rest of society. Those issues are very well described in these books. And I don't think many people are aware of what many Latino families go through or are dealing with.

Throughout my experiences with Lucero, I found myself trying to discern how much critical and cultural awareness she held. She was a tad older than the rest of the Latina teachers but harbored a youthful demeanor and optimism that she shared through her frequent laughter and jovial manner. I was, however, mindful of being respectful of her boundaries during our interactions. I was never quite sure how introspective (i.e., criticality-wise) she was about racial and cultural issues. More specifically, I was not sure about how she positioned herself and her role within the greater context of racial issues – which is to say, I'm not sure she was fully aware of her power to navigate and help students navigate cultural intersections (i.e., among Black and Latinx cultures). I came to believe that much of what I was likely perceiving was due to her faith and the way in which she sought to view individuals from a humanistic stance (though I questioned whether such a stance might be deficiently color-neutral).

Upon first moving to Alabama, Lucero expressed how confused she was about the racial biases she witnessed and experienced. She recalled microaggressions such as being asked if she knew any cleaning ladies that could clean houses (i.e., during her employment at a majority Black middle school), or how people automatically assumed that she enjoyed eating spicy foods. She expressed how she grew to understand that the color of her skin signified that she was not to be trusted, particularly in White retail spaces, where shopping without her White husband usually involved showing extra forms of identification and answering more questions. She also recounted a story about when she was teaching Spanish at a predominantly White upper-class school (a school that would later not renew her teaching contract) – she explained how she couldn't understand why her young Kindergarten students wouldn't repeat the word for the color "black" on the board. "Negro." She tilted her head back and laughed during our interview upon remembering how, after a few minutes, a little boy said, "African American" and it dawned on her that the word she had written on the board was misperceived as a racial slur.

During our last conversation, upon being asked about the biases that all people carry and the type of biases she might carry about her predominantly Black students, she expressed the following:

Society permeates who you are, but you have the power to influence society. And it's like you are going against the river – it's always trying to push you, but you fight back. I know biases exist and are there, but I'm constantly fighting them.

# Mercedes' Testimonio

They never ask for my opinion,
they never ask for what I think –
> they never ask probably because
> they think I don't have
> the right to say anything or
> I don't have the right to say
> anything as an outsider.

I'm not from Alabama,
they don't consider me to be an American
> because I don't speak English
> like they do.
>> And because I'm Latina,
>> I'm neither White nor Black.

I have had administrators
mock my nationality and
colleagues who have made
horrible comments about
Puerto Ricans.

[But] my mother did not raise quitters.

Tu eres la unica que puedes
definir tu identidad.[3]

I am a social defender –
my culture influences everything
in my life.

My language is part of my identity,
it's part of who I am.

Defiende lo que crees y
se leal contigo misma.[4]

Use your voice, don't let others silence you.

I was so excited about meeting a Puerto Rican teacher in Alabama. It hadn't dawned on me until I was driving up to the large rectangular gazebo at the public park close to Mercedes' house, that I had never met another Puerto Rican teacher during the 15 years I lived in Alabama. Upon meeting Mercedes, I swiftly remembered why I had been so excited – she immediately started speaking Spanish and I immediately realized how much I had yearned to inter-act and hear the language and accent that represented Home. Unlike my prior reservations and self-consciousness of speaking "correct" or "fluent" Spanish with Lucero, my Spanish-speaking anxieties dissolved and were replaced with the relief of being able to easily share our Puerto Rican dialect.

Even now, as I reflect and begin writing Mercedes' testimonio, I can't help but become teary-eyed at remembering our first encounter. She had been patiently waiting for me inside a large pearl-white pick-up truck that belonged to her friend. Her car had broken down and she had asked her friend to bring her to our meeting and wait for our interview to end. She asked me what most Puerto Ricans ask each other upon first meeting – "De que parta de la isla tu eres?" (From what part of the island are you from?). I typically approach this question with self-doubt about my Puerto Rican authenticity, since I solely lived on an Army base close to San Juan for six years of my life (i.e., though my entire family is from Puerto Rico and most of my extended family still resides in the Greater Metropolitan Area of San Juan). Thankfully, Mercedes didn't skip a beat and simply affirmed my response – "Oh, Ft. Buchanan!"

After our general introduction, Mercedes began completing a pre-questionnaire prior to the commencement of our conversation. She looked up and asked if I wanted her to respond in English or Spanish and I responded that she could write in whichever language she felt most comfortable. She then verbalized that she didn't really have any expectations of the original study, but quickly corrected herself as if the thought had been waiting to be spoken aloud – "Sounds weird, I've got no idea of expectations. I've got no expecta-tions of this [study] . . . well, I've got a voice. I've got a voice for many Latinos living in this part of the United States." And, just like that, and from what seemed like that moment forward, Mercedes continued to articulate issues, sentimientos/feelings, thoughts, perceptions, and knowledge in a seemingly effortless way – it's almost as if she had a knack for condensing monumental sentiments into concise and digestible words and phrases. During our last con-versation, I actually asked her about this, about whether she was aware of how easily it seemed like she was able to articulate immensely complex thoughts – shockingly, she said, "No."

From our first conversation, Mercedes was quick to express how devoted she is to her family. Despite her parents divorcing when she was four years old, she remained close to both parents throughout her life. She cared for her mother when she became ill during Mercedes' 11th grade year in high school and later during college. Mercedes quit school for a year to work but attended night school to make up her 11th grade and returned to finish high school and graduate with her 12th grade classmates. When I asked about her family,

Mercedes described how her father was born and raised in Puerto Rico and how her mother was born and raised in New York but moved to Puerto Rico when she was 14. She described how her paternal family "came from a poor resource background, all raised in public housing" and how her mother "came from the middle class." Her mother was a teacher, "but had to work three jobs to be able to maintain us." She attributed her parents' divorce "possibly [to] the differences in their social status."

She expressed how she had always wanted to become a teacher because her mom was a teacher. Just like her mother, who Mercedes described as a warrior, she began studying to become a special education teacher in Puerto Rico. She taught special education while she studied but moved to Alabama where she expected to finish her teaching degree. Upon moving to Alabama, however, she made the decision to pursue Spanish as her teaching field:

> Before I started in Special Education, I decided to switch to Foreign Languages because of my language problem. I thought that although I wanted to major in Special Education the [students] would notice that I had a language accent, which would not have been fair to them or me. So, I decided to change my major to Spanish. It was very hard; my first semester was extremely hard, very difficult. The English I knew came from Puerto Rican public schools and I only had basic vocabulary. Although I had a lot [of basic vocabulary], I could not express myself properly with that vocabulary. It was very difficult, but the love I had for education convinced me that I could do it.

It's important to note that Mercedes' responses were predominantly in Spanish, though she occasionally spoke phrases and sentiments in English. Mercedes stressed how difficult it was for her to complete her teaching degree in Alabama, due to the English texts and reliance on the English language. She described this experience as her "greatest cultural shock." She described how she went from being a straight-A student in Puerto Rico, to failing courses in Alabama. She would spend entire days at the college library translating her textbooks, without any support from her instructors or the university – "They didn't think I had the mental capacity, but it was an issue of language, not capability."

It was right after her first year studying in Alabama that her father gave Mercedes full custody of her 14-year-old sister, who had special education needs. While completing her Spanish education degree in Alabama, Mercedes also periodically cared for her mother, who was ill with cancer. Mercedes is, without a doubt, a fierce survivor – as she likes to say, "My mother didn't raise quitters."

Throughout our three conversations and three book pláticas, it also became clear how proud and culturally sensitive and intuitive Mercedes is about her heritage –

> I think that being Puerto Rican we grow up with a hybrid culture, with the pain of being a colony. Puerto Rico has never been a republic, it has always been a colony and, as such, we have a cultural pain, a cultural depression. We have a longing for the rest of the world to learn our story, our history. [When Puerto Ricans] arrive in the States we are [no longer] Puerto Rican, [we] are not White, [we] are "Latino," or Mexican. So, we have different identities. I will always be Puerto Rican, but for the world I'm a Latina, Hispanic, or whatever the world decides for us to be, or how they identify us.

Mercedes expressed her passion about teaching and how she gains continued inspiration from her students. She described how she actively seeks ways to learn more about her students because she knows how cultural connections make for lasting relationships with her students. Such connections also made it possible for her students to be open to what she teaches – especially when she teaches the nuances of Latinx cultures like Afro-Latinx customs. She came across as a self-learner who is committed to learning about her students to be a better teacher. She is the type of teacher who attends her students' baby showers and weddings long after they have graduated from her high school Spanish classes. She described herself as easy-going and happy – llena de ternura (filled with tenderness). She also expressed a heightened sense of awareness and described how everyday she has felt "violence, abuse, and maltreatment" for being Latina. She stated the following:

> As teachers we make a lot of mistakes due to our biases because we come with the romanticism that we learned about the world, about American history, Latin American history, the romanticism of colonization, and all that relates to being an American, including patriotism. We've forgotten that there are other different versions of history. I have to be [aware] because we're in Alabama, because [racial and cultural differences and prejudices] are the norm of the culture in the community in which we live. My opinion isn't important in how I teach, because I don't teach my opinion. I simply teach the bridges. I try to have effective questions, but my students' opinions are their opinions and I can't influence their opinion – I can only teach about [overall] different opinions that exist.

Despite Mercedes' sense of social understanding and awareness, she tended to hold herself back when it came to communicating in English, often questioning her skills and abilities because she felt insecure about her command of the English language – "It's just that I don't feel completely comfortable with English. Creo que es un poquito de complejo, de fragilidad (I think it's a bit of a complex, of fragility)." It was often personally painful for me to witness when Mercedes expressed these insecurities, since she was so articulate and incredibly expressive in Spanish. Interestingly, during the book pláticas, Mercedes took her time forming her opinions, sometimes compelling the other two collaborators to interrupt her or finish her sentences. During our individual conversations, however, when left to talk with minimal interruptions, she eloquently put into words the most complex ideas.

From our first conversation, Mercedes expressed concerns about meeting in person, due to the pandemic and an underlying health concern she harbors. So, while she attended our first conversation and first book plática in person, she engaged in the remaining conversations and book pláticas remotely via Zoom. For this reason, I also dropped off supplies and picked up completed tasks from her home on her porch. It was during one of these visits to her home that she gave me a tour of her large backyard garden with several composts and detailed plans for continued growth. These visits also allowed Mercedes to show her giving nature and our budding confianza/trust – on one occasion she gave me a bottle of homemade Puerto Rican hot sauce and several pasteles (i.e., Puerto Rico's version of tamales, that are often made with love and eaten during special occasions like Christmas). For me, these offerings symbolized ties to Home, culture, confianza, and friendship.

## Conclusion

The narratives that Consuelo, Lucero, and Mercedes shared helped me to contextualize what might happen when we, Latinas, are forced to accept a certain constraining reality that suffocates the cultural life we carry inside, day after day. It is like a seemingly gentle steam bath, where the heat slowly and invisibly expands the body's pores to absorb the suppressive and oppressive elements surrounding our yellow, bronzed, and brown bodies. The body doesn't notice it at first – it's not the kind of otherness that might smack you in the face like scalding water. For the three Latina teachers, their narratives expressed a cultural pain and yearning to be Home, a place where they remembered belonging. Just because we Latinxs cannot always verbalize our pain or the ways in which America has sought to suppress our unique cultural identities and constrain our bodies in assimilationist and colonized bondage, this doesn't mean we don't constantly struggle to carry the burden of being othered because of our Latinidad. Just because, for example, the shade of our skin, texture of our hair, or fluidity of accents may not match our level of cultural awareness, doesn't mean that we carry a hefty degree of grief within our bodies. We may not be consciously aware of our cultural pain, but it still lingers like the pain of a phantom limb.

The testimonios featured in this chapter are a testament that the lived experiences and truth-narratives of Latina teachers matter. All three teachers engaged in sharing their stories by way of connecting to the young adult literature out of a desire to no longer be invisible or ignored, but to be seen. They chose to share intimate details about their lives to shed light on their experiences as Latinas, as teachers, as Latina teachers. The first thread of the testimonios were poems created from the teachers' sentiments. The second thread comprised the testimonios, during which I drew on my own Latina experiences and cultural intuition to identify emerging themes like familia/family, empowerment, and belonging. The following chapter delves into the themes that emerged from the testimonios, including the subthemes of being grounded by familia (especially strong mujeres and impactful mothers, and stories of cariño y amor [care and love]); the otherness, grief, and yearning to home tied to belongingness; and empowerment connected to teaching Spanish, being bilingual, and a heightened awareness and understanding.

# Notes

1 I reference "Home" with a capital letter "H" because of the importance it holds in Consuelo's life (and the other collaborators' lives).
2 Never stop being who you are, don't give importance to your accent ... that accent is what makes you unique.
3 You are the only one who can define your identity.
4 Defend what you believe and be loyal to yourself.

## · 4 ·

# CULTIVATING THE EXPERIENCES OF LATINA TEACHERS IN THE DEEP SOUTH

Humans are symbol-users, creatures *born to* use the gift of language, *storytellers* from the very origins of articulation. We learn from accounts of our experiences, and from the experiences of others, by exploring *the language* that shapes and guides *the storying* of those experiences. The more natural the story, the easier it is to read – and to get close to, or identify with – the facts and the feelings of what is being said. The more closely we can narratively identify with the facts and feelings, the nearer we are to getting to an experience of *truth* in what is being said. (Goodall, 2000, p. 194)

Much like Goodall's (2000) description about storying above, the language and storytelling of the young adult literature texts and the teachers' experiences shaped several overarching themes. The more the teachers and I read and shared, the more readily I was able to discern the feelings, truth, and knowledge that the teachers were making and expressing. This chapter delves into the themes and subthemes that emerged. Specifically, the following themes and subthemes will be explored: familia/family – grounded by familia, including strong mujeres, impactful mothers, and narratives of cariño y amor; belongingness – otherness, grief, yearning for home; and empowerment – teaching Spanish and being bilingual, awareness, and understanding.

# Findings: Themes and Subthemes

One of the main themes that centered the narratives that Consuelo, Lucero, and Mercedes shared was the importance of familia/family and how familia, particularly strong mujeres and stories of cariño y amor (caring and love), grounded each of the collaborators. Another predominant theme that emerged was the centrality of belongingness, or lack thereof, tinged with emotional stories about being othered, experiencing grief that stemmed from linguistic and racial violence, and yearning for Home. The final overarching theme became evident via stories about empowerment that stemmed from teaching Spanish and being bilingual, an increased sense of awareness, and an understanding of the collaborators' surroundings and spaces that they shared with predominantly non-Latinxs. The remainder of this chapter will examine each of these themes and corresponding subthemes. These themes and subthemes were prominently centered at the core of each collaborator's cultural and lived experiences. For each of these themes and subthemes, information relative to each of the collaborators' stories will be integrated to support the themes. It is important to note that while I will present distinct themes and subthemes that represent the narratives that the Latina teachers shared, oftentimes these narratives converged with each other, blending distinctions to comprise fluid stories about the Latina teachers' culture. The themes and subthemes, however, serve to highlight the nuanced and multidimensional attributes of the narratives shared by the teachers, thereby rejecting a monolithic view of what it means to be Latina (and Latina in the Deep South).

## Grounded by Familia/Family[1]

The prominent role of family was ever present during the conversations and book pláticas – from Consuelo's description of aguacates/avocados from her tía's yard that were so delicious you could eat them "with the peel and everything," to Lucero's accounts of singing alongside her mother while they cooked warm arepas in her childhood home of Barquisimeto, Venezuela, to Mercedes' recounting of summers spent swaying in a hammock and smelling sweet mangoes and piñas at her grandmother's pineapple farm in Puerto Rico. The book pláticas further heightened the role of family. All of the young adult literature (YAL) texts centered the Latina protagonists within the context of their Latinx families. Thus, the narratives about protagonists' identities and journeys to self-discovery about their hybrid identities often prompted the teachers to share stories about their own families and the role their families had on their own identities. I remember, for example, how Consuelo (who was initially guarded) first shared intimate details about herself by recounting how Xiomara's mother in *The Poet X* (Acevedo, 2018) reminded her of her own mother who was critical of her, but also carried the weight of doing and maintaining everything in the household. She expressed how she found herself becoming more like her own mother, how she had shifted from being more adventurous in life to more cautious.

Similarly, Lucero described how Julia's mother in *I'm Not Your Perfect Mexican Daughter* (Sanchez, 2017) reminded her of her own mother, in that both were constantly working and sacrificed their time and labor to provide for their families – "My mother didn't work outside the house, but she was constantly working." Like Julia's mother, who taught her the value of earning money by taking her to clean houses, Lucero's mother taught her the value of contributing to the household by teaching her how to cook – "[Julia's mother] would bring her daughter to clean the houses with her. Well, my mother would pull me out, 'Okay, let's go, you're going to help me cook.' I learned how to cook because my mother taught me how to cook. She was working constantly – everything, cooking, cleaning, doing whatever needed to be done in the house. [It wasn't until] after my mother passed when we saw everything that she did."

This first main theme of being grounded by family was anchored by the subthemes of having and benefiting from strong mujeres and impactful mothers, in addition to stories about cariño y amor (caring and love). Below I will explain how these subthemes emerged from the stories that the collaborators shared during their interviews and book pláticas.

## Strong Mujeres and Impactful Mothers

Consuelo, Lucero, and Mercedes consistently shared stories about the women in their families, particularly their mothers. Stories about mothers who expected college degrees and demanded greatness, mothers who instilled a firm work ethic by modeling tireless sustenance of their familias, and mothers who held strong boundaries of safety, abounded. All three shared a convergence of experiences regarding boundaries that were placed on them by family but enforced by their mothers. Specifically, after reading *Knitting the Fog* (Hernandez, 2019), all three empathized with the main character, Claudia, whose mother would not allow her or her sister to visit friends outside of school without proper supervision, thus inculcating a sense of over-protection by family. For example, Lucero recounted:

> I feel like [Claudia]. I identified with Claudia, from her childhood, the type of education, the relationship with her mother. The mother being very strict – [my] mom would not allow us to play with our neighbors at all, [saying,] 'No, they say curse words; I don't want you to listen to those curse words.'

Both Consuelo and Mercedes shared how their mothers never let them stay at the homes of their friends, with Consuelo remembering her mother's words, "I prefer [your friends] here, you're not going anywhere." It occurs to me now that neither me nor my Latina friends ever had sleepovers because all of our mothers shared the same sentiment – that is, friends could come stay at our house, but we weren't going anywhere.

During one of the book pláticas, when I asked the teachers whether their families were matriarchal like those of the three YAL books we had read, they all agreed. While there is a common perception that many Latinx families are led by machista (i.e., hyper-masculine) heads-of-households, Consuelo, Lucero, and Mercedes provided unique perspectives. Consuelo succinctly expressed how the women in her family were strong because they had to be strong. She recounted how her maternal grandmother raised her six children on her own because, "my grandfather was out of the picture early because he was a drunk. He was [like] the guy in the book, drunk." And because her father was periodically deployed in the military, her mother raised her and her siblings. Lucero attested that "my father thought that he had the pants, but my father would say something, and my mom would override it. So, we would ask permission from my father and tell my mom to convince him. My mother would get the permission regardless." Mercedes also expressed how her "dad was in the military [reserves] all his life, but my mother was a Nuyorican, you know, so . . . she was a very strong woman."

All of the collaborators' mothers were also persistent about the value and attainment of a college education. Consuelo's mother insisted that before she joined the Army, she had to earn a college degree – she recounted how her mother told her, "Once you give me that piece of paper with your name on it, then you can go do whatever." Similarly, Lucero recalled how her mother, who could always be found reading, stressed the importance of education:

> Especially for my mother, education was always very important. [She would say,] 'Your job is to go to study.' We were four sisters and six brothers – I'm the youngest

of the sisters. For my family, especially for my mother, education was always very important. All my siblings were first generation college [students].

Mercedes followed in the footsteps of her mother to become a teacher. She expressed how close she was to her mother:

[My mother] worked very much. We did not share too much time during the day, but we were very close. Whenever I saw my mother, she was everything to me; all I wanted was to be with her because I hardly saw her.

Later, Mercedes expressed how her mother was "un motor" (a motor/catalyst) in her life – "she's been a warrior." In fact, Mercedes attributed her mother to encouraging her to finish her education degree in Alabama – "I would spend all day in the library translating all my books. I kept on trying because my mother kept telling me that she did not raise quitters, that I had to keep at it."

## Stories of Cariño y Amor (Caring and Love)

Consuelo, Lucero, and Mercedes shared numerous stories tinged with cariño y amor. These stories included a reciprocity of receiving and giving cariño y amor from and to their families. Expressions of cariño y amor were marked, for example, by having high expectations and minimizing monetary and household distress. Consuelo expressed how her mother, tías, and abuela always wanted more from her:

We [my siblings and cousins] were all raised by women. So, they always said, "You can do better if you want to do better. But it's on you if you want to do more." They'd say, "I will do this, but you have to do [your part]."

Both Consuelo and Lucero also recalled how their parents were experts at minimizing any monetary struggles the family was experiencing. During one of the book pláticas, Consuelo commented, "I know we didn't have money. There was a time there that my dad made $11 a month. We never knew." Lucero responded by saying, "And my father would go for months working somewhere. Your parents kind of shielded you from that." All of these sentiments were expressed within the context of sharing stories based on questions posed about the YAL texts we read. For example, the responses above regarding monetary struggles were elicited after the collaborators were asked, "What was your reaction to the hunger and poverty in the book? How did that make you feel? Did it remind you of any of your students or your own background?"

Both Lucero and Mercedes also recounted deep devotion toward and caring of their family. Lucero recounted how she had temporarily paused her college education in medical school to care for her mother for two months, who had suffered a heart attack and later died. It was this experience that solidified her decision to pursue biology and biology education, rather than medical school:

> I love to know all the science, of the anatomy, the biology of the body and all that. [But] I realized that I didn't like the practice. I [couldn't] see myself in the hospital. I didn't want to . . . I can't bear the pain, to see other people in pain.

Mercedes also recounted caring for her sister (for whom she took full custody when she was 24 and in college) and her mother during her initial diagnosis and reoccurrence of cancer. In addition, she also volunteered to care for her father, who suffers from leukemia, and who will likely be moving to live with her in Alabama.

All three teachers reminisced about homes filled with love by way of music, food, and singing, in addition to outdoor experiences drenched in freedom and rugged nature. Lucero described how her home was always filled with music – "Music is in my DNA." She recalled an uncle who would "come every weekend to play with his band," in addition to music and singing "that was just part of life, singing while you were doing chores. I'm cleaning, we are singing. We are cooking, we are singing . . . no occasion at all, just part of life." Similarly, the outdoors acted as a form of freedom and recollection of love during childhood. During the third book plática while discussing *Knitting the Fog* (Hernandez, 2019), I asked about any personal memories that were brought up by the book. Consuelo quickly recounted how the main character would visit the local junkyard to find treasures – this reminded her of a wood-dumping area close to where she lived in Maryland where she and her siblings would swim in a river. Mercedes then described how the description in the book of mangos and tamarindo/tamarind trees reminded her of her grandmother's pineapple plantation in Puerto Rico. During our first conversation, Mercedes also recalled "memorable times while living in an era when everything was free as a child, without fear of anything happening to you," among a "very united family."

## Summary of Being Grounded by Familia

The overarching theme of familia, in addition to the subthemes of being grounded by familia and strong mujeres, and childhoods filled with cariño y amor were ever present in the narratives of the three Latina teachers. These recountings, particularly of cariño y amor, represented by stories and memories of family interactions, scents, locations, and sentiments provided a multidimensional representation of how family grounded the three teachers. This theme and subthemes aided in conceptualizing how knowledge about familias and Latinx backgrounds contribute to humanizing and contextualizing the experiences of Latinas in the Deep South.

## Belongingness

The stories of belongingness reminded me how we, Latinas living in non-Latinx spaces, have spent so much time pretending that we're the same, somehow, as those around us, that we forget or resist questioning the fissures of cultural instability surrounding us. We brush off how we're rarely asked for our opinions. We stop trying to be at the table of change, since our voices are shunted, ignored, or overlooked. When we finally start realizing that this invisibility is far from normal, it seems like it might be too late to make changes – we only have so much time before we retire or move on, so we continue to swallow our pride, we become more settled into the background, like fragmented and opaque bits of ourselves within a white-washed gelatinous mold. Except, when we don't or won't accept the tolerance of discomfort or invisibility. The book pláticas helped dislodge our collective silence – they offered a space to affirm our unique Latinidades, our individual experiences, identities, and relationship to culture and language. They also contributed to sharing collective and individual knowledges about our experiences. The Latina teachers shared parts of themselves – truths born of roughened terrains dimpled by divots and crevices that represented their lived experiences, experiences that branded their embodied selves. The theme of belongingness encapsulated Latina cultural authenticity and American cultural authenticity – no matter if they had an accent or not, if their skin inhabited varying shades of burnt umber, their sense of otherness, grief of linguistic and racial trauma and violence, and yearning for Home and belonging remained ever present throughout the study.

The three YAL texts that guided the book pláticas included predominant themes of assimilation and cultural authenticity (i.e., both Latinx cultural authenticity and American cultural authenticity). Markers of American authenticity were encapsulated by way of education, citizenship status, and English fluency. Latinx cultural authenticity was exemplified via the protagonists' identity-journeys – via their accents, skin color, body shaming, religion, rites of passage (e.g., quinceañeras), and tensions surrounding assimilation.

Language was a source of much discussion for the three teachers. Stories about language were tied to identity, power, shame, and authenticity. Mercedes recalled how language was tied to her identity and has remained a source or renewed authenticity –

> My language is part of my identity, it's part of who I am. Yes, [my] accent changed, [my] vocabulary changed. I think mi Español es mas amplio, mi Español es mas rico, compared to when I first got [to Alabama.] Even though I was already in college, I still needed mas conocimiento y vocabulario. I feel like my accent [in Spanish] changed, pero sigo arrastrando/dragging my r's and l's. I try to modify them when I'm talking to students, when I'm talking with you all, when I speak to other people – I try to make sure my accent, the characteristics of Puerto Rican Spanish, no sean tan marcadas [aren't so marked]. But when I speak with Puerto Ricans, hablo "arrastrao" – I feel happy. I love speaking Spanish. It's part of who I am. It's part of my identity.

While Mercedes' Spanish has altered to make room for a version of Spanish that is suitable for teaching, her Puerto Rican Spanish remains steadfast. Interestingly, Mercedes mentioned how she made sure to unmark her Puerto Rican Spanish characteristics, even during our book pláticas, which led me to believe that she likely felt a mark of judgment regarding her Latinidad. Lucero also mentioned how:

> My Spanish has suffered. And I don't have my Venezuelan accent anymore – because I have so many Mexican students and from Central America, that now "el andale" comes out. The last time I went to Venezuela, the Consul, they asked me, "Where are you from?"

## Stories of Being Othered

Upon discussing the main character, Claudia, in *Knitting the Fog* (Hernandez, 2019), Consuelo, Lucero, and Mercedes expressed how language had, at some point in their lives, been a source of otherness. For Lucero and Mercedes, it was tied to their English-speaking abilities, while for Consuelo it was about speaking Spanish in Mexico. Lucero explained how she related to Claudia by how she felt criticized for speaking English – "I still, I mean, [students] still make fun of me because of my accent. And [they] try to speak like I speak English, like mocking [me]." She would, in turn, remind them that they too have accents when they speak Spanish. Mercedes also identified with Claudia –

I feel like I identify with [Claudia] based on my own fear of English. I'm not sure if it's because I've suffered a lot of discrimination because of my accent here in Alabama. It's difficult, especially from the beginning when you try to go to a fast food [restaurant] and you go through a drive-through and people don't want to hear you. They don't want to take the time to understand what you're saying. [For example,] when people try to make you feel uncomfortable, asking you like many times –"What!? What!?" And you know they understand. Things like that make me feel really uncomfortable and insecure with the English language.

Conversely, Consuelo expressed an opposing experience with Spanish, not English – "Mine is the opposite. When I go to Mexico in the summer, they know I'm not from there. I may look like them, but I ain't from there." She proceeded to explain how her vocabulary in Spanish was not as extensive as her English vocabulary – "I basically think in English." Consuelo also explained how she had grown up with the incongruence of a melting pot mentality, despite recognizing her Latinidad – "When we grew up, you grew up under that umbrella of, 'We're all the big melting pot.' So, everything . . . we were assimilated into. There was no [such thing as] being different." Additionally, Consuelo expressed how she had never felt like an insider, not at work or professionally. Even with her friends, she expressed, "With my friends, sometimes they don't realize how they sound, like [Mexicans] are all supposed to like enchiladas, we're all supposed to do [specific things]." She further explained how different Alabama is and how tiresome it is to have to explain cultural attributes to others. Even seemingly simple actions like growing up with open doors and friendly neighbors, highlighted her stories of otherness in Alabama and how she always felt the need to explain cultural attributes –

You have to start over with a story, with the explaining. It's like, "Look, we didn't grow up that way. We grew up where it's like your door was constantly open. People were constantly coming in." I moved here to Birmingham and neighbors don't talk around here.

Lucero's stories of otherness were primarily expressed via stories about a lack of teacher support, to include professional development, even when she sought to better her teaching craft by seeking National Board for Professional Teaching Standards (NBPTS) certification. She recalled how she approached an assistant principal and principal to ask for help to fund her NBPTS certification. And while her administrators supported her, the district ignored her emails and requests for support. Lucero expressed the following:

I want professional development, I want to learn more skills to teach Spanish, but they are not offered or if they are offered, the district doesn't make any effort to make it available for any Spanish teachers. I guess because we are foreign language teachers. The district isn't interested because we don't teach English, Science, or Math. These are the [subjects] they're interested in because they are vulnerable because of [standardized] testing. As a Latina, I just don't think that we make any difference.

Lucero's sentiments are indicative of existing tensions of being othered due to the teaching field of Spanish being considered an elective, which is perceived as second best, as non-essential. This becomes further problematized upon considering that many foreign language teachers, particularly Spanish teachers, are likely Latinx or have ties to Latinidad. For Lucero, moving from Venezuela (where people are racially mixed) was difficult. She expressed having a very hard time negotiating the intricacies of race in America –

So, coming here and seeing the labels, for me, I never understood why there are so many races, why I'm not any of these . . . because I'm not White, I'm not Black, I'm not Indian. Ethnicity, Latino, Hispanic, whatever . . . it's too much. I just don't want to label. It's what I don't want. I just want to be, this is Lucero the human being, with no labels.

Similar to Lucero, Mercedes also acknowledged how in Puerto Rico, despite there being differences regarding skin color and biases, most Puerto Ricans view themselves as Puerto Rican, not via multiple racial categories. She expressed these sources of otherness and how they resulted in multiple hybrid identities as follows:

I'm Puerto Rican and I'm a White Puerto Rican. Let me explain what happens. Yes, we have a double identity because, well if you are a Puerto Rican in Puerto Rico you are a "Boricua", you never say you are Latina. You are simply Puerto Rican and ignore there are other Puerto Ricans who are Afro-Puerto Ricans. You ignore it [the racial distinctions] because of the privilege that exists in the world. I'm not referring to politics, but how it exists in the world, and how the color of your skin is perceived, particularly between being white or light skinned which dominates the world. It dominates the politics, the economy, it dominates all. So, we do not differentiate between those skin colors because we do not understand [we are color-neutral], nor do we live by that. It is only when we arrive here [in the U.S.]. Until you arrive in the States and [then] we are not Puerto Rican, you are not White, you are "Latino", or Mexican. So, we do have different identities. I will always be Puerto Rican. But for the world I'm a Latina, Hispanic, or whatever the world decides for us to be, or how they identify us. I had never thought about all of this until recently, even when I arrived here or a few years after. I did not understand a lot of things. I could not understand why other cultures saw me differently. Even among Latinos, they see us differently. Why Puerto Ricans do not embrace other cultures and why do other cultures do not accept us? I believe this is a consequence of Puerto Rico being a colony. If you only speak one language you have information from that point of view. However, if you have information in English, which is the dominant language in the world, it is quite broadening. So, when you start getting information from other sources you awaken. So, yes, we do have lots of identities. We have the identity of how you see yourself and how you are seen.

Both Consuelo and Lucero also shared how they resisted being labeled, particularly being labeled as Latina teachers in their schools. During the second book plática Consuelo expressed the following:

If they say it doesn't matter whether you're Hispanic or Black, then why do they always ask? Why do they always bring it up if they say it doesn't matter? It shouldn't matter, I should just be a teacher. I want to be seen as a Latina woman, but not a Latina teacher. Because I am a teacher.

Lucero responded by stating, "[Being a] teacher is [being a] teacher regardless, [whether] you're Latina or whatever . . . Chinese, Hispanic, or whatever. I think [being a] teacher is [being a] teacher, why should it matter [to be labeled as a 'Latina' teacher]?" I had initially begun to suspect that perhaps Consuelo and Lucero had internalized dominant White norms of assimilation in a way that was negating (or subtracting from) their Latina identities. Coincidentally, Mercedes expressed a different perspective –

Hay muchos maestros que son Latinos, pero que no se exponen. Tenemos que hablar y estar orgullosos de lo que somos y presentar nuestra cultura; es necessario porque la diversidad es importante. Porque nosotros podemos enseñarles cosas que otros maestros no pueden enseñar, otra visión, abrirles el mundo.[2]

What I grew to understand and empathize with, was that the term "Latina teacher" is viewed within a confining and monolithic context without acknowledging the nuanced cultural attributes that represent the multi-dimensionality that encompasses being Latinx or Latina in America. Thus, being labeled as a "Latina teacher" in Alabama may be akin to being racialized (with racial violence) in a deficit manner. The teachers featured in this book are not only Latina, they are also Spanish teachers – they inhabit double racial targeting at predominantly non-Latinx schools. Kohli (2018) reminds us that schools can perpetuate hostile racial environments for teachers in the following ways:

... schools are institutions that historically and currently have been designed to create and maintain racial inequality. The racism that exists occurs on structural, macro levels, which include policies, infrastructures, and schoolwide practices that maintain the racial status quo, as well as on the individual, micro levels such as personal and peer interactions that are racially charged. Together, the macro and micro manifestations of racism form a climate that is racially hostile to teachers of Color, particularly those who advocate for racial justice. (pp. 314–315)

These examples gave voice to the stories the teachers shared about how their multilayered identities and intersectionalities of race, language, culture, and skin color converged to make them otherized (Lynn & Parker, 2006) or other in predominantly non-Latinx spaces in the Deep South. Mercedes summarized feelings of otherness as follows:

Yo creo que nosotros los maestros Latinos nos sentimos un poquíto olvidados, un poquíto olvidados, un poquíto separados. Hay veces que sentímos que no pertenecemos en ninguna de las dos comunidades, asi que estámos en el aire, estámos en el limbo, estámos en el medio de todo pero no pertenecemos a nada. Estámos en el mismo medio del huracán, entre los vientos que no se mueven.[3]

These sentiments of otherness primarily encompassed how Consuelo, Lucero, and Mercedes didn't seem to neatly satisfy the dominant perception of what it means to belong within a predetermined category of Latina or Latina-American. For Lucero and Mercedes, since they are not Mexican, they don't fit into being Black, White, or Mexican – the primary categories that appear to prevail in the Deep South. For Consuelo, despite being Mexican, she did not embody the stereotypical perception of Mexican in the Deep South – that is, she is a professional educator with no accent, married to a Black man, who is independent and served in the military. The collaborators voiced stories and expressions of otherness tied to their Latinidad, their skin color, accent, and teaching subject matter.

## Stories of Grief

The first time I remember hearing a story tinged with grief, I was uncertain if the word "grief" accurately described the sentiments being shared. The more I continued looking at the totality of stories shared by the teachers, however, the clearer it became that concepts or words like "racism" were insufficient to describe the essence of the stories shared by the collaborators. These stories comprised the grief, trauma, and violence that comes from experiencing and witnessing racism, exclusion, and invisibility.

Consuelo recalled a stark and baffling experience upon first moving to Birmingham, when she was at a bank and was bluntly asked, "What *are* you?" She recalled feeling confused about the question, since she had never been asked this question before. During both of the individual in-depth interviews, Consuelo also stressed how she didn't recall ever feeling like an insider. This was not, however, specific to the Deep South, since it also included the many places she had lived throughout her childhood and Army career. She recalled living in Texas, where she calls Home, during her freshman year of high school and a counselor telling her that she should pursue teaching, "because of her situation." She asked, "What if I want to be something else?" and she recalled him saying that because she was Mexican, she should pursue teaching. This is what made her initially resistant to pursuing teaching as a profession, despite her love of languages and skill at teaching during her Army career. Such microaggressions also contributed to why she decided to give her daughter an Americanized name rather than the name she desired, Consuelo, "because nobody would be able to say [her] name."

Lucero described how she believed that her heavy accent while speaking English, in addition to her dark-colored skin, contributed to her teaching contract not being renewed in a predominantly White, upper-class school district in the Greater Metropolitan Birmingham Area of Alabama. She indicated that she would not have thought the non-renewal decision was based on her Latinidad, had it not been for colleagues who confirmed that the reason was likely racial.

Out of the three teachers, Mercedes shared the most searing account of grief. She recalled how after the 2016 presidential election of Donald Trump, her predominantly Black students became increasingly hostile toward her and the other Latinx students at her school. During our first individual interview, she described how her Black students began ridiculing and mimicking her accent, which had not happened before. She experienced serious disciplinary problems with her students – "Something that I could not understand because I was one of the best-liked teachers at the school." She described how she had sought support from a White assistant principal at the school who asked Mercedes to prove her claims "and kept walking." She also recounted the following:

> Those first two years with the change of the national government, well, my students would make fun of me, would mimic my accent. It was horrible. I would call the parents; in the past I had a very good relationship with my student's parents . . . very good communication for many years. I did not understand why [the students] would act that way. I used all my knowledge of classroom management, my knowledge of

cultural issues, of assimilation, well, of everything. Everything I've learn from all the books I've read, everything, every tool. They were violent. At one point they made me cry. I was very depressed and asked them if they mimicked other teachers, other Afro-American teachers. I told them that what they were doing was racist, that it was racism. By mimicking someone who is not from your same racial background, [this] is considered racism. They were in shock and began to film me [on their cell phones]. I continued talking and told them to go ahead and record it. I told them that every morning I come with love, asked them when I had ever offended them. I asked them, "Why are you mistreating me? Why? Because I'm not White or Afro-American? That is racist." They were in shock but kept on recording.

Mercedes proceeded to describe how the week after students recorded her, one student ended up physically pushing her. She sought the assistance of an assistant principal, who called the student's mother and upon learning that Mercedes had called the students racist, chose to not take disciplinary action. The student returned to Mercedes' class as if nothing had occurred. Mercedes described how she handled the situation:

The assistant principal never called me. Two days after I went to the assistant principal and told him that the student had returned to my classroom, he told me that he needed to talk to me. The assistant principal and the student are both Afro-American. So, he tells me to sit in his office. Because of my accent I tend to be very timid and for many years I was the outsider, the one that would not complain, keeping quiet about problems. But this time I said to myself, no more. So, at the office the assistant principal says the student is in your classroom because you called him a racist and you cannot accuse a student of being racist. I told the assistant principal, "You're Afro-American, so how would you feel if it was you in the classroom, imagine with all White students and they mimic your accent. How would you describe it?" He opened his eyes widely. I told him, "I would call it racism, what would you call it?" He opened his eyes widely and said he did not know they were doing that. I told him that I had expected him to call me into his office so I could defend myself, but he did not give me the opportunity to do so. As far as I know I'm the only Latina teacher in this school, "So, what can you call what happened?" Since that meeting with the assistant principal, he does not have anything to do with me. He left the school for a while but [later] returned. However, he keeps away, basically being very formal with me, addressing me as Mrs. Mercedes. But I have not forgotten that he did not give me the opportunity to defend myself. So, now you have a generation of students that believe that it was me who was wrong. We're talking about 160 students that I teach in a semester. Students that were this [student's] friends, [they] probably all believe that I was wrong.

I have shared this extensive excerpt from Mercedes' story as an exemplar of the racial and linguistic violence and trauma that has been inflicted, resulting in an overwhelming sense of grief. All three teachers continue to navigate racialized experiences as Latina educators in the Deep South. Kohli (2008, 2014) has high-lighted how teachers of Color have "been educated by an oppressive schooling system that promotes white [or White European] cultural values, and oftentimes we are socialized to see non-white cultural knowledge as inferior to that of the dominant culture" (2014, p. 372). Thus, teachers of Color can internalize racism and unknowingly repeat "racial hierarchies" (Kohli, 2014, p. 368). Consuelo and Mercedes are the sole Latinx teachers at their schools, while Lucero is one of two (i.e., there is another Latino ESL teacher, a Latina secretary, and several Latinx custodial workers at her school). Their sense of grief appeared to stem from being the sole Latina teachers in their schools, of feeling overlooked and powerless at times, and of a yearning to be seen for who they are.

## Stories About the Absence and Yearning of Home

The last book plática culminated with feelings of familiaridad/familiarity among the teachers, and a sense of vulnerability resulting from the text (*Knitting the Fog*, Hernandez, 2019). Both Lucero and Mercedes expressed feelings of cultural pride that were infused with yearning. Lucero explained how, "you leave part of your soul in your own country" when you leave. She described how if you are not an immigrant you cannot understand this feeling of loss. Lucero was still yearning (and grieving) having left Venezuela, especially since the current political situation has prevented her from visiting Venezuela. In fact, she had not been to Venezuela for seven years, having to infrequently visit her siblings in neighboring Columbia. The protagonist in the YAL text entitled *Knitting the Fog* (Hernandez, 2019), Claudia, expressed this sense of absence and loss in a way that Lucero was able to relate, thus heightening her own emotions. These emotions were made evident during the book plática. She expressed how some immigrants who do not really want to leave their country often feel "arrancados" or yanked from their homes – "I wish I could [return to Venezuela]."

Mercedes also expressed evidence of a multilayered sense of cultural con-sciousness and new mestizaje, where she appeared to describe "a tolerance for contradictions" (Anzaldúa, 1987, p. 101), in this case the contradictions embodied a cultural pain and necessity to remain in Alabama. She expressed the following:

> I always feel melancholy about Puerto Rico. I miss Puerto Rico every single day. I feel that I am here, but my heart and soul, my brain, my mind is in Puerto Rico, you

know? Estas aqui, pero quieres estar en otro sitio.[4] It's like I wish I could go back, but I can't right now. I wish someday I could return to Puerto Rico, but I cannot right now. And I think we live with that pain. It's like a pain. It's like when you've lost something. Grieving. That is how I feel all the time – that is very sad, but it's very true. When you asked us about [our] language and I [said] my language is my identity, it's because I feel closer to the island, to my culture, to my family. I speak Spanish because it makes me feel more comfortable, of course, and I feel closer to my culture, my identity.

During the second altered book experience, Mercedes described how she had drawn a tree that represented her cultural roots – "I have a big tree here because ... this is my tree, this represents my roots and it also represents my family. Las raices representan cual fuerte son mis raices y por mi tierra y por mi isla."[5]

Consuelo also frequently indicated how Alabama was not her home, even after having lived in Alabama for 20 years. In describing one of her altered book creations, she recalled, "I'm just trying to find a place to call home. Even though I've been here twenty-something years, Alabama is not my home." During the first book plática, she also expressed wanting to leave Alabama – "Still, I want to get away ... I still want to get away. You know, sometimes I just want to get in my little car and just keep going somewhere. You know? Just go. Just get in my car and just run somewhere." She also stressed how she intended to return to Texas, to her Home, after she retired. Consuelo's yearning to return Home was also marked by how difficult it has been for her to hold on to her culture, particularly in instilling the Latinx side of her children's ethnicity –

Assimilation, it's easy to do that – it's really hard to hold on to your culture when you're the only one [here]. And I say that [partially] because of raising my kids, when we got [to Alabama], there weren't a lot of Hispanics, so there weren't too many places to find [Latinxs] to really teach [my kids about Latinx culture]. So, the only time they really got [Latinx culture] is what little bit I would put out during the week, during the year. And then we went home [to Texas] in the summer; and we would stay all summer.

## Summary of Belongingness

The theme of belongingness was one of the strongest threads throughout the narratives shared by Consuelo, Lucero, and Mercedes. Being the sole Latina teachers at their schools was bounded by feelings of being diminished, overlooked, and invisible. Each teacher harbored Latinx distinctions that served to otherize them in their schools and communities. For Consuelo, it was her physical Latina attributes of darkened hair and brown skin. For Lucero it was her thick English accent and darkened skin. For Mercedes, it was her thick English accent. This sense of being othered because of their identities and their Latinidad, attributes they cannot hide or change, appeared to result in a heightened sense of grief, including linguistic and racial violence. Home has remained a yearning absence that has been kept alive by a pained and embodied attachment and sentimiento dentro del alma (feeling within the soul).

## Empowerment

I have purposely chosen to end this thematic section of the chapter with the broad theme of empowerment, to conclude with sentiments of hope, power, and healing. I define empowerment as an increased sense of agency, connection, and confidence within and outside the self. More broadly, I borrow Anzaldúa's (2015) expansive definition of empowerment -

> Empowerment is the bodily feeling of being able to connect with inner voices/resources (images, symbols, beliefs, memories) during periods of stillness, silence, and deep listening or with kindred others in collective actions. This alchemy of connection provides the knowledge, strength, and energy to persist and be resilient in pursuing goals. Éste mode de capacitar [this mode of capacity] comes from accepting your own authority to direct rather than letting others run you. (pp. 152–153)

Teaching Spanish and being bilingual were centered as ways to connect with Latinx culture and pride. In addition, stories about heightened awareness and understanding of Latinx culture, and cultural value in general, appeared to be tied to hope, healing, and cultural persistence (i.e., despite racial violence and going against the proverbial current of being the sole Latina within predominantly Black and White spaces). Consuelo, Lucero, and Mercedes indicated that the three YAL texts, in addition to the book pláticas and conversations allowed them to, as Consuelo stated, come "back to the roots" of being Latina – "So now, it's like I'm changing, trying to go back and say, 'I get who I am.' You really can't move forward without knowing who you are." At the final book plática, all three expressed how the entire experience had allowed them to think more broadly about stereotypes toward Latinxs and, as Mercedes expressed, "thinking about my identity, it's difficult, it's interesting."

The teachers were also able to share moments of convergence when the pláticas brought up different terminology that was similar to or different from their Latinx cultures. For example, when Lucero recounted how a section in one of the books reminded her of how her mother used to bathe her in a washbasin, all three participants organically shared their version of the term "washbasin" – a "pila," a "pileta" a "batéa." This particular moment turned into a beautiful description of Lucero's mother bathing her outdoors in Venezuela and Consuelo's mother similarly bathing her daughter when she was a toddler in Texas.

## Stories About Teaching Spanish and Being Bilingual

All three teachers have taught Spanish for over 13 years. All three also came to teach Spanish for different reasons, despite Spanish not being their initial first choice of content to pursue in teaching. When I first learned that Consuelo, Lucero, and Mercedes were Spanish teachers, I am ashamed to admit that I assumed they taught Spanish because they were Latinx. I was feeding into a confining, constraining, and deficit perspective about Latinx teachers in non-Latinx teaching spaces. While I did not immediately believe they taught Spanish because it was easy (or easier) for them, I did pre-judge them based on stereotypes about Latinas predominantly teaching Spanish and/or English as a Second Language in Alabama. This prejudgment quickly shifted to awareness and respect when I learned about their stories and how teaching Spanish and being bilingual provided a unique opportunity for empowerment via teaching about Latinx cultures – that is, to "school" their kids on the realities and nuances of Latinx cultures. Below, I recount some of the narratives that the teachers shared.

Consuelo had initially rejected pursuing teaching as a profession after an unfortunate experience with a high school counselor when she was a freshman. That counselor had expressed microaggressions by telling her she should pursue teaching because of her circumstances and because she was Mexican. That is, he presented teaching as a lesser profession. Consuelo, however, chose to follow her passion for languages and facility with teaching. She indicated that she taught Spanish to break down and "get rid of all those [negative] stereotypes [about Latinxs]." For the third altered book task, Consuelo also depicted her superpower as language – that is, her bilingual abilities, coupled with her sense of adaptability and flexibility. She recounted how language and being bilingual equates to power – "There's power in [being bilingual]."

Lucero expressed how she acknowledged the rewards of teaching Spanish –

Because I am Latina, the students from Spanish speaking countries they can see in
me someone that they can talk to, someone they can relate to. So, they come, even
though I don't teach them, they come to me. They greet me in the hallway, "Buenos
días Señora Lucero, como está?"

When asked about her relationship with or to language, Lucero quickly
responded, "Well, I love being bilingual! My Venezuelan accent has changed,
but . . . it's powerful to be bilingual. Because I speak Spanish, I understand
Portuguese, I understand Italian. I can read French, [but] I cannot speak
French. I just love language!" Lucero also shared expressions of empowerment
in being able to teach Spanish culture and situating Spanish culture within
the context of her students' cultures. By focusing on Spanish culture, Lucero
is also able to understand the importance of learning about other cultures
as well. This understanding also makes her more aware of the biases that
everyone carries and how she must continue fighting against her own biases
as they arise.

Mercedes frequently described how she was passionate about teaching and
was enlivened when teaching Spanish. She recounted how Spanish has given
her the opportunity, "to not only teach Spanish as a language, but also culture
in all of its aspects, in relation to the community – to teach about the [Lat-
inx] community and its culture." In fact, Mercedes and the two other foreign
language teachers at her school have begun researching how to establish a
Foreign Language Academy at her school, so that she can expand upon the
Spanish course offerings to include Spanish Literature and sociocultural issues
(e.g., like a series of ethnic studies courses). Mercedes also frequently emphasized how language, specifically her Spanish language, is part of her identity.
Additionally, Mercedes expressed how teaching the cultural aspects of Spanish
physically brought her joy and energy –

Cuando yo enseño mi cultura, tengo una sonrisa de oreja a oreja y mis estudiantes lo
notan. Entonces yo me siento felíz cuando enseño a mis estudiantes. Creo que ellos
me dan la energía – cuando yo estoy ensenañdo yo soy felíz.[6]

Teaching Spanish has also allowed more freedom of creativity in how
Consuelo, Lucero, and Mercedes teach their content. Since it's not a content
area that is rife with standardized testing, they are able to incorporate creative
and artistic strategies, so long as they meet their teaching and curriculum standards. Teaching Latinx culture has also made them more aware about other

cultures, in general. This knowledge has empowered them to learn more about their students' cultures – as Mercedes highlighted:

> Lo mas importante es conocer la cultura de quien tu estás enseñando. Lo más importante es conocer a quien tu le enseñas, conocer sus problemas sociales, conocer su historia. Hacer preguntas ... es necesario hacer preguntas, es necesario exponer, aprender de esa nueva cultura donde estás entrando.[7]

## Stories of Awareness and Understanding Leading to Hope and Persistence

Consuelo, Lucero, and Mercedes shared narratives about being and becoming aware – of heightening their awareness about sociocultural issues and what it means to be Latina (and a Latina teacher) in the Deep South. Their stories progressively expressed a deeper understanding about their hybrid identities and how their "geography of selves" were composed of "diverse, bordering, and overlapping countries" (Anzaldúa, 2015, p. 69). In some instances, such as when Consuelo and Lucero resisted being labeled as "Latina teachers" at their schools (and instead emphasized being Latina women who are teachers), they began "pushing against any boundaries that have outlived their usefulness" (Anzaldúa, 2015, p. 75). In essence, while they could not yet explicitly name it, their stories exhibited navigating the cracks of nepantla (i.e., between cultural worlds), leading them toward a "hybrid consciousness that transcends the us versus them mentality of irreconcilable positions" (Anzaldúa, 2015, p. 79). Additionally, their stories also reinforced their increased sense of conocimiento (consciousness) – that is, their awareness appeared to be heightened by their "surroundings, bodily sensations and responses, intuitive takes, emotional reactions to other people and theirs to [me], and, most important, the images [their] imagination [was creating] ... deepening the range of perception" (Anzaldúa, 2015, p. 120). The more we met, together and individually, the more it became evident that they were navigating through (e.g., backwards, forwards, simultaneously, and in isolation) some of the seven stages of conocimiento that Anzaldúa (2015) described as: el arrabato (a jolting awareness); nepantla (liminal and in-between space); Coalique (desconocimiento or temporarily wandering away from awareness); the call (crossing into action); putting Coyolxauhqui together (transforming oneself again); the blow up (testing clashing realities); shifting realities (transforming and forming alliances).

During Consuelo's first conversation, she expressed not really having focused on her identity or Latinx culture, likely because of being raised by an ultra-patriotic military family and her own eight years spent in the Army. She later recalled how this bubble of a quasi-melting-pot-mentality contributed to her choosing to ignore her differences. By our second conversation, however, Consuelo had begun articulating how she had never had to think about her racial identity. She recounted how she used to react to issues and how that had begun to change:

> I'm trying to think of the conversations I have with my [children]. I listen to them, how they mix-in the culture and stuff like that, but I just never really thought about me doing that. Now, [this study] has made me more aware of that. It's like all of a sudden, I'm seeing more of what's out there and how others view me. Before, I just let it all fly over, not even think[ing] about it. Now, my feathers get ruffled up. Now, it's like, "Why do you say that? What do you mean, 'those people'?"

Consuelo went on to describe how her daughter, whom she calls an activist, had been speaking to her during the spring of 2020 about the Black Lives Matter Movement, and had been criticizing her for her lack of awareness. She recalled the following – "My daughter the activist, she's like, 'See Ma, where have you been?' I was like, 'Well, until somebody shows you, you don't know you're not seeing things. Until somebody tells you, you don't know that.'" Upon being asked what types of support she would like to see as a teacher, Consuelo responded as follows:

> Well, they're trying. Well ... no, they're not. [We need] more cultural awareness, because the majority [of teachers] are African American – you have more of those kinds of professional development. You have more of those kinds of examples put into professional development. You have to be aware that color doesn't just mean Black or White. You've got all those brown shades in the middle too. I didn't realize how bad it was, honestly. I'm telling you, this [study] is probably better for me than it is for you. I know it's going to help you get your Ph.D. and everything, but for me, it's really opening my eyes to a lot.

By the last book plática, Consuelo had also begun questioning forms of cultural appropriation by reconsidering how she would teach cultural aspects of el Dia de Los Muertos (the Day of the Dead), a theme she has taught every year in November –

> The word I pulled out [from the third book] was changing, coming back to the roots, because I never really used to think about who I really was, I was just me. I'm [now]

staying away from the [Dia de Los Muertos] sugar skulls, I'm staying away from, you know, all the little colorful things and [instead] really focusing on what is the meaning of it. Why is that so important to remember who you are and where you came from? Because even here in the States, people don't ever think about who they are or where they came from, they just are. And I picked up a lot of that too. So, now, it's like I'm changing, trying to go back and say, "I get who I am." And really, now that I think about it, you really can't move forward without knowing who you are. That's what I tell my students ... how do you know what you're going to do [in life] if you don't know who you are, who you're becoming?

Lucero expressed the importance of lessons that she had gained from reading and discussing the three YAL texts. She described this importance as follows:

The books raise awareness of what the Latino community is going through in this process of trying to fit in and the process of why [Latinx families] are here – the struggles with the language and culture shock. There is [also] the issue of adapting to or accepting a new culture and trying to incorporate that culture into your life, because you want to fit in with the rest of society. Those issues are very well described in these books. And I don't think many people are aware of what many Latino families go through or are dealing with.

Interestingly, from the first conversation, Lucero had expressed how she had never really internalized a dual or hybrid identity, however, upon moving to Alabama (i.e., the United States), she had been forced to racialize her identity. She explained how her faith and studies in biology had allowed her to be cognizant of the oneness of humanity that we all share, no matter our ethnicity or cultural practices. Upon being asked how she identified racially or culturally, she responded as follows:

I identify as a Latina because I was born and raised in South America, and I guess, the way we were raised, what we eat, how we dress, how we relate with other people, I guess is part of the Latina culture. I travel a lot and I have learned from other cultures, and I have learned respect and understanding from other cultures, especially because of my faith, because it's a faith that is based on looking for the oneness of humankind, the Bahai faith. Understanding and loving the differences of everybody, so, regardless of race, regardless of identity, cultural identity, regardless of even religious background. I always thought, well, we're all human beings. We might look different, but we are all human beings. People, I mean, there are big differences, but we are living on the same planet, we are breathing the same air, we're all eating the same food, we are looking at the same sun. We just look different, and we might have a different education, but we all are the same. I mean, we are just human beings. Biology tells us, we're all just human. Even, the taxonomic classification of the human being is there is just one. The only problem actually came when I came here, because in Venezuela we don't talk about race. The type of prejudices are a little different.

Throughout the study, Mercedes provided narratives about having a heightened awareness and understanding of her Latinidad and about general sociocultural issues related to Latinxs and African Americans. She shared the following:

> [Having many identities] is an asset because if you can see different points of view from different sources, it is an advantage. It is a privilege. It's an awareness. You start to understand where you come from. As teachers, we make a lot of mistakes due to our biases because we come with the romanticism that we learned about the world, about American history, Latin American history, the romanticism of colonization, and all that relates to being an American, including patriotism. We've forgotten that there are other different versions of history. Hay muchos maestros que no quieren ver los problemas sociales. No se abren a ver que estan llenos de prejicios.[8] I am Latina, but I'm Puerto Rican and I benefit from some privileges that I have within the Latino community. Also, I'm "blanquita" (White) and I benefit from that as well. That is the reality ... until I talk [English], "de ahi se terminan los beneficios" (and that's where my benefits end).

Mercedes also expressed her own limitations as a Latina in Alabama and how she came to realize her limitations within the Latinx community in Alabama. She expressed this as follows:

> Honestly, I think I've had less experiences with the Latino community [in Alabama], with the exception of the Puerto Rican community. I think I've had less opportunities to interact with them, to understand more of other Latino cultures firsthand, other than what I have read. I think [the book pláticas] have made me think more, based on the questions asked, because before I think we take things for granted – of the fact that I'm Latina, but what does it mean to be Latina, how have I been involved with the Latino community? I am Latina, but what do I know about my Latino community? Am I really Latina, or am I Puerto Rican?

This example highlights how Mercedes gained insights from reading and discussing the YAL texts at the book pláticas. It also sheds light about how she had begun cultivating a "cultural sensitivity to differences" – that is, intracultural sensitivities (Anzaldúa, 2015, p. 81). She appears to be beginning to "forge a hybrid consciousness that transcends the 'us' versus 'them' mentality" and potentially "bridging the extremes of our cultural realities," that is, via a "nos/otras position" (Anzaldúa, 2015, p. 81).

## Summary of Empowerment

The broad theme of empowerment, of increased agency, confidence, and confidence, was evident in the stories the teachers shared about teaching Spanish and being bilingual and gaining an increased and heightened sense of awareness and understanding. In fact, all three expressed an increased sense of awareness and understanding of the spaces they inhabit in the Deep South (i.e. both within and outside of their embodied selves or geography of selves). From Consuelo realizing that she had begun putting "a lot of [cultural] FYIs out there" to let her students know "that there's more out there, and not to be so close-minded," to Lucero self-affirming how she had been "doing the right thing in raising more of this [cultural] awareness in her classes," the increased awareness and understanding appeared to be empowering and hopeful. These stories and attributes of empowerment served to broaden a sense of healing, hope, and persistence among the teachers, which they emphasized sharing with their students. They sought to continue learning about their students' culture in order to bridge further inter- and intracultural understanding during their focus on Latinx culture in their classes. As Mercedes wisely observed:

> My Latino students and my African American students have much in common. They have more in common than what they see – so, I show them. That is my job – to highlight "cuan parecido somos, que compartimos" (how similar we are, what we share).

## Conclusion

As the testimonios, individual conversations, and book pláticas conveyed, the teachers' narratives embodied a collective culture of seeking belongingness despite feeling grounded by family and empowered by Latinidad. Home is kept alive by a pained and embodied attachment . . . dentro del alma (within the soul). Despite having come to teaching Spanish for alternate reasons, for all three teachers, teaching Spanish was a convergent thread that became a source of empowerment because it gave them an opportunity to teach Latinx cultural nuances from their voice and perspective. It also allowed them to challenge deficit and negative stereotypes about Latinxs, in addition to bridging unity and commonalities among and within other cultures (i.e., including intracultural exploration of the various Latinx cultural attributes represented by the teacher's and YAL character backgrounds). Teaching Spanish, however, also remained a source of being othered, given that the subject/content area isn't deemed as necessary or valued, particularly in a high school setting (i.e., where the stakes are higher, and core academic content areas are integral to graduating and being accepted into higher education). Another convergent thread was that all three teachers expressed feeling othered because they were in primarily non-Latinx spaces where being Black or White (and possibly Mexican) were the only seemingly acceptable silos of recognition and quasi-acceptance.

The three overarching themes that emerged from the stories told by the Latina teachers encompassed family, belongingness, and empowerment. Specifically, the thematic threads and sub-thematic threads appeared to be prominently centered at the core of each teacher's cultural and lived experiences, as expressed in their stories and encompassed in the following:

- The centering of familia/family and how the teachers' familias, especially strong and impactful women and stories of carino y amor (caring and love), grounded each collaborator.
- The centrality of belongingness, which was marked with stories about being otherized, experiencing grief resulting from linguistic and racial violence, and an absence of and yearning for home.
- The relentless surge of empowerment that stemmed from teaching Spanish and being bilingual, which resulted in an agentic increase of cultural awareness and understanding that appeared to result from the teachers' interactions within and among predominantly non-Latinx spaces.

Thus, the stories shared by the teachers exemplified narratives of their authentic selves that were interrupted to recreate and broaden narratives of their Latina individuality. The following chapter examines what we can learn from Latina teachers, to better retain and support them as professionals and unique individuals who have brilliance to share based on their beautifully complex backgrounds. When Latina teachers are encouraged to explore who they are and how they show up in the world, much can be learned from and about them. Given that the population of teachers continues to remain overwhelmingly White, and that students of Color continue to grow in public schools across the United States, the final chapter delves into implications and discussion of the findings in the book.

# Notes

1   Throughout this chapter and chapter four, I will refer to "family" by interchangeably using the words "familia/family," "familia," and "family."

2   There are many teachers that are Latinos, but they don't reveal themselves [as Latinos]. We need to speak up and be proud of who we are and represent our culture; it's necessary because diversity is important. Because we can show them things that other teachers can't, another vision, open them up to the world.

3   I think that we, Latino teachers, we feel a bit forgotten, a bit forgotten, a bit separated. There are times when we feel like we don't belong to either of the two communities [Black or White], so we are in the air, we are in limbo, we are in the middle of everything but we don't belong to anything. We are right in the middle of the hurricane, within winds that don't move.

4   You are here but yearn to be someplace else.

5   The [tree] roots represent how strong my roots are for my land, my island.

6   When I teach my culture, I have a smile from ear to ear and my students notice. Therefore, I feel happy when I teach my students. I thnk they give me energy – when I teach, I am happy.

7   Of utmost importance is knowing the culture of whom you teach. It's most important to know who you are teaching, know their social problems, know their history. Asking questions . . . it's necessary to ask questions, it's necessary to expose yourself, to learn about that new culture into which you are entering.

8   There are many teachers that don't want to see social problems. They do not want to open themselves to see/realize that they're full of prejudices.

# · 5 ·

# Y AHORA QUE? WHAT CAN WE LEARN FROM LATINA TEACHERS?

This book explores the lived experiences of three Latina teachers in the Deep South by using three young adult literature (YAL) texts (written by Latinas) to bridge and guide expressions of the Latina teachers' stories and experiences. The literature surrounding Latina teachers in southern states like Alabama is scant, as is the literature regarding the use of Latinx YAL texts as sources of knowledge from which to explore the lived experiences of Latinas. The study upon which the book is based encouraged me to explore my own sense of cultural alienation and invisibility that permeated my 15 years of living in Alabama while working at a predominantly White institution of higher education. Through this book, I was able to begin personally reclaiming my Latina agency and liberating myself from a colonized and assimilationist mindset. As Anzaldúa (1990) urgently reminded me:

> We cross or fall or are shoved into abysses whether we speak or remain silent. And when we do speak from the cracked spaces, it is con voz del fondo del abismo[1], a voice drowned out by white noise, distance, and the distancing by others who don't want to hear. (p. xxi)

I endeavored to "collectively share experiences, while establishing a sense of community" (Flores & García, 2009, p. 155) by facilitating a space to engage in three book pláticas to center the multiplicity and multidimensionality of Latinidad. "While there are many similarities and differences among and across our Latinidades, there are also complexities that stem from our differences" (Flores & García, 2009, p. 168) – the YAL texts aided in situating the complexities and multifaceted aspects of being Latina in the United States, thereby providing a platform from which to plásticar and collectively share the Latina teachers' lived experiences. Thus, this book also complicated and problematized Latinas as a monolith by exploring the identity-narratives of Latina narrators and the lived experiences of Latina teachers who represented varying Latinidades (i.e., both the narrators and teachers represented different Latinx cultures).

The Latina teachers critically engaged with YAL and discussed how they did or did not identify with Latina characters who represented varying Latinx backgrounds similar and different than their own, thereby illuminating ways in which cultural practices and notions of Latinidad are fluid and socially constructed. Thus, the YAL characters may be reflective of both windows and mirrors among the Latina teachers. The YAL also invited the Latina teachers to consider various perspectives "beyond those informed by their cultural identities" (García & Gaddes, 2012, p. 152). This book does not presume a monolithic Latina narrative and instead explores the Latinx YAL for complexities of racial/ethnic identities and backgrounds (Sciurba, 2014). Much like the third space (Gutierrez et al., 1999) created in the García and Gaddes (2012) study, the study for this book relied on the use of texts and translanguaging (e.g., the use of Spanish and/or English) to create a space where the participants could rely on their Latina identities as a "mediational [or interventional] tool" (p. 161) to critically examine their lives in relation to YAL characters and themselves (i.e., Latinas representing different Latinidades).

## Discussion of Research Inquiries

### What Perspectives Do Latina Teachers Share About Their Personal and Schooling Lived Experiences in the Deep South?

The Latina teachers shared myriad stories about their personal and schooling lived experiences. These stories were inclusive of being grounded by family, yearning to belong and be home, and developing a heightened critical awareness that was hopeful and empowering. The stories the teachers shared grounded them in their current roles as teachers in Alabama. In particular, being grounded by family appeared to give the collaborators strength, tenacity, and persistence to continue teaching. Their perspectives and stories about their lived experiences consistently centered the role of strong mujeres/women and impactful mothers who inculcated the importance of education and dedication. As Sanchez and Ek (2013) remind us, "The tools of *educación*, passed on from mother to daughter, will only rise in importance as more and more Chicanas/Latinas pursue formal education" (p. 183). Stories of cariño y amor (tenderness and love) abounded in the perspectives and narratives that the teachers shared.

Consuelo, Lucero, and Mercedes also shared various personal and schooling experiences about the greater theme of belongingness by sharing stories about being othered at their schools for being the sole Latinas and/or Spanish teachers, in addition to personal experiences of yearning for their cultural homes, despite having lived in Alabama for many years. This yearning for a cultural home and refuge, in addition to feeling like an outsider and not belonging is not unusual. Yet, the sentiments are raw, pain-filled, trauma-induced, and gaping. Anzaldúa (2015) describes this experience as tension-filled and disorienting:

> While juggling several cultures or forces that clash, nepantleras live in tense balances entremedios [in-between], teetering on edges in states of entreguerras [within wars]. We're not quite at home here but also not quite at home over there . . . stuck between the cracks of home and other cultures – we experience dislocation, disorientation. (p. 81)

The teachers also shared various empowering personal and schooling experiences that were tied to teaching Spanish and being bilingual. Teaching Spanish and being bilingual contributed to the collaborators' sense of agency, particularly in their non-Latinx teaching spaces where they were the sole Latinas and/or Spanish teachers at their schools. They also shared countless stories that exemplified personal and schooling examples of heightened cultural awareness and understanding (e.g., wanting to continue learning about their students' cultural backgrounds to better teach them about Latinx cultures).

More specifically, in spite of Spanish being viewed as a less important subject area than the core academic areas (e.g., Math, Science, and English), the Latina teachers nonetheless embraced and celebrated the agency they wielded by being able to teach Spanish through their pride-filled lenses.

They demonstrated different forms of community cultural wealth (Yosso, 2005) including the following forms of cultural capital:

- linguistic capital – includes the "intellectual and social skills" (p. 78) gained through communicating in more than one language/style; the teachers fully embraced and celebrated their Latinidad by engaging in Spanish as a profession
- familial capital – refers to "cultural knowledges nurtured among familia that carry a sense of community history, memory, and cultural intuition" (p. 79); the teachers reinforced their unique Latina identities by integrating their own experiences, metaphors, stories, and anecdotes of Latinidad into their Spanish curriculum
- navigational capital – involves the "skills of maneuvering through social institutions" (p. 80), including academic spaces; the teachers learned to navigate predominantly non-Latinx spaces where they were often the sole Latinxs by celebrating Latinidad via their Spanish culture curriculum
- resistant capital – refers to "oppositional behaviors that challenge inequality" (p. 80); the teachers recounted stories during which they explicitly dismantled negative and deficit-based stereotypes about Latinxs during their Spanish lessons – that is, teaching Spanish afforded them opportunities to embed asset-based perspectives and nuances when they taught about culture.

## How Do the Teachers Describe Their Lived Experiences as Related to Young Adult Literature Written by Latinas?

The three YAL texts can be classified as multicultural texts, critical texts, or social justice texts, however, they are most succinctly defined as Latinx YAL, since García's (2017) description below holds true:

> . . . Latinx literature for youth functions as a counter-canon to both U.S. and Latin American tropes and norms. Today's Latinx authors for youth challenge the kind of internal and external racism, sexism, and classism that has rendered Latinxs invisible in U.S. and Latin American literature and society. (p. 117)

All three texts centered strong Latina protagonists who "challenge[d] and transform[ed] the different forms of violence they experience[d] in their lives" (Rodriguez, 2019, p. 9). Such challenges and transformations aided in facilitating stories and counter-stories that the teacher collaborators consistently shared during the book pláticas. Each of the YAL texts contained protagonists who negotiated a journey toward self-discovery and self-identity. These journeys situated navigating assimilation and cultural authenticity – that is, both American authenticity and Latinx authenticity. American authenticity was marked by traits such as English fluency, citizenship status, and independence from family. Latinx authenticity was marked by traits such as speaking Spanish, body shaming, colorism, and cultural rituals like quinceañeras.

*Knitting the Fog* (Hernandez, 2019), for example, provoked many discussions among the three Latina teachers about being othered because of language issues. The protagonist, Claudia, moves to Los Angeles from Guatemala at age 10. Claudia struggles tremendously to fit in and learn English and assimilate. Both Lucero and Mercedes recounted several painful and trauma-filled experiences in Alabama with students mimicking and mocking their accent when speaking English. Mercedes also recalled how denigrating it was to endure people who purposely asked, "What!? What!?" in restaurant drive-thru speakers. All three collaborators also recalled how their Spanish had changed and shifted from having taught Spanish for so long. Unlike Claudia, whose mother chastised her for using Mexican slang, however, Lucero and Mercedes shared loving accounts of using phrases that their Central American and Mexican students used. Consuelo also recalled how her Spanish was criticized for its lack of authenticity when visiting Mexico – that is, she wasn't viewed as sufficiently Mexican during her summer visits to Mexico.

The YAL texts and corresponding book pláticas were essential in providing a meaningful platform that centered Latinas, in addition to Latinx YAL themes such as strong family relationships including intergenerational family interactions, cultural assimilation and alienation, and questioning authority "from the dually marginalized position of both a young person and a racial and ethnic minority" (García, 2018, p. 234). The sentimientos/sentiments and expressions that the teachers shared about being othered, mostly evoked from pláticando at the three book pláticas, appeared to encompass the ways in which they appeared to reject dominant (mis)perceptions of what it means to be Latina in the Deep South (and likely, the United States as a whole). All three teachers appeared to become increasingly more aware about sociopolitical issues related to being Latinx in America. Much of this increasing awareness appeared to be primarily attributed to the YAL texts. Additionally, their sense of understanding about themselves and their students of Color appeared to increase as well. On several occasions, Lucero expressed how the

YAL texts allowed her to better understand her students and motivated her to continue implementing nuanced cultural content in her Spanish curriculum. While it is not necessarily surprising that the YAL texts led to collaborative meaning-making among the collaborators, Latinx YAL texts have the continued ability to expand upon the knowledge base surrounding Latinx communities and sources of Latinx empowerment. Rodriguez (2018) reminds us that, "Reading realist fiction in Latina/o children's and young adult literature through the lens of conocimiento narratives [or a Latinx critical lens] further presents the opportunity to discuss the ways Latina/o children can process institutional racism, patriarchal violence, and xenophobia, for example" (p. 63). The YAL texts and book pláticas provided the teachers with a healing space where they engaged in moments of pain, joy, and conocimiento . . . all facilitated via "healing alternative narratives" (Sosa-Provencio, Sheahan, Fuentes, Muniz, & Vivas, 2019, p. 212) or counter-stories exemplified in the YAL. Further, the YAL texts and book pláticas reinforced "healing-centered engagement" (Ginwright, 2018) by centering Latinx culture and collective healing (i.e., as a researcher-participant, it was my goal to create a healing space via our discussions and the YAL texts).

## What Can We Learn from Latina Teachers Through Their Personal and Schooling Lived Experiences?

The stories and perspectives that the three Latina teachers shared throughout this study were compelling and offered essential points from which to learn. Most importantly, what we can learn from these stories is that they reinforce the need to better understand Latinas as unique individuals within a broader pan-ethnic view of Latinidad. Even more broadly, these stories remind us that we must solicit and pay closer attention to the stories of all teachers of Color.

The stories that led to the emergence of the theme of belongingness appeared to exemplify the ways in which non-Latinx individuals might inadvertently enact linguistic and racial violence against Latinxs (i.e., consciously or not, purposefully or not, intentionally or not). The stories that highlighted lack of belongingness, being othered, experiencing and internalizing grief, and yearning for a cultural home of refuge, stressed the importance to be better informed about Latinxs with whom we share space. Schools have traditionally been places of oppression for students and teachers of Color – the time is ripe for school cultures that fortify diversity and nurture community.

The stories that led to the theme of empowerment highlighted the teachers' sense of vigilance regarding their surroundings. While they often felt overlooked and misunderstood at their schools, they were also deeply committed to their students, particularly regarding how they teach culture within their Spanish curriculum. This aspect gave me a deeper appreciation for how Spanish teachers (and other culturally aware Latinx teachers) likely have much to contribute in the area of incorporating intracultural and intercultural aspects and endeavors into the school's culture, professional development for other teachers, and within the teaching curriculum for all subject areas.

Providing spaces where Latinx teachers can continue to explore their lived experiences and congregate to bear witness and support each other, is especially important in geographic areas like the Deep South, where Latinxs are a growing minority in predominantly non-Latinx places. Calderon et al. (2012) remind us that "Women united in close circles can awaken the wisdom in each other's hearts. If in addition we learn to surrender to the ancestors' guidance, we will learn about our mission together." (p. 534). Thus, for example, affinity groups at the K-12 level, in addition to teacher education programs and induction programs (e.g., critical professional development via teacher inquiry groups [Pour-Khorshid, 2016]), should be an established norm. For example, spaces like the Latinas Telling Testimonios (Flores & Garcia, 2009) and Somos Escritoras/We Are Writers (Flores, Batista-Morales, & Salmerón, 2019), where groups of Latinas converge to explore their unique and intersecting identities – healing and hope-filled spaces to celebrate the joy of Latinidad, and to examine the pain and embrace the healing resulting from institutional racism that seeks to oppress our Latinidad. National groups like the American Educational Research Association's Hispanic Special Interest Group or the American Association of Hispanics in Higher Education could unite in their efforts to disseminate such affinity group spaces.

## Moving Adelante

The findings in this book relied on LatCrit and Chicana/Latina Feminism. I relied on these frameworks to explore the lived experiences of three Latina teachers by utilizing, among other methodological approaches, testimonios imbued with muxerista portraiture. These frameworks and approaches guided the book by allowing me to shed light on the teachers' experiential knowledge and lived experiences via a loving gaze aimed at reframing them as educators from whom to learn, as empowered and resourceful educators. Additionally, these frameworks, and the resultant findings from the original study, allow for the possibility of many positive changes within K-12 schooling and teacher education programs. Such possibilities include, for example, increased retention of Latinx teachers, in addition to a broader exploration of diverse perspectives and culturally affirming understanding of content/curriculum for students from multiple ethnicities.

## Implications for K-12 Schooling and Teacher Education Programs

The "Latinization" (Irizarry & Donaldson, 2012, p. 156) of K-12 schools is ever present and increasing, given the continued growth of Latinx students in our public schools, who comprise 26 % of students of Color (De Brey et al., 2019). Teachers, however, remain overwhelmingly White, with only 9 % being Latinx (De Brey et al., 2019). And while grow-your-own programs and other forward-thinking recruitment plans have been successful at recruiting more teachers of Color in public schools, "minority teachers [including Latinx teachers] have significantly higher turnover than White teachers" (Ingersoll et al., 2019, p. 1). These turnover rates are primarily a result of job dissatisfaction comprising working, organizational, school administration, and "instructional autonomy" (Ingersoll et al., 2019, p. 31). Moreover, in a study that centered Latina Spanish teachers, Colomer (2014) found that, "When Latina Spanish teachers knew they were supported, whether by the institution they worked for or by an outside agency, they were more likely to expand cultural and social capital and more willing to establish networks with Latino students" (p. 362).

This book underscores the need to better understand Latinx teachers in order to empower, support, and retain them, particularly in predominantly non-Latinx spaces with growing Latinx populations like the Deep South. Specifically, in 2019 Latinxs comprised 18 % of the U.S. population (up from 16 % in 2010), and the broader area of "the South" included half (48 %) of the Latinx population (Krogstad, 2020). Some of the fastest growing counties in the U.S. (since 2007) were in Georgia, Alabama, and Louisiana (Krogstad, 2016), with Alabama ranking as number five in overall Latinx population growth in the U.S. between 2000 and 2014 (National Council of La Raza, n.d.). The Latina teachers in this book expressed stories of being otherized and overlooked, of not being invited to the proverbial table – in this case, they were infrequently included at any tables that represented power at their schools. Understanding the experiences of Latina teachers (and all teachers of Color) can help build retention, solidarity among Latina teachers (and teachers of Color), collegiality among all teachers, and increased opportunities for mentorship and support.

In this book, the Latina teachers did not feel included in a school community – on the contrary, the stories they shared highlighted feeling like outsiders. Administrators at public schools undoubtedly have myriad federal, state, and local district agendas to meet and may not realize the importance of the cultural inclusion of their teachers, and how efforts toward inclusion will trickle down to students. Despite their implicit or complicit ignorance of the institutional and structural racism and oppression that foregrounds schooling in America, it is negligent for administrators to be hesitant, resistant, or ignorant about implementing culturally relevant and culturally sustaining pedagogical practices for their students *and* teachers. Continued opportunities for teachers to explore their cultural values and professional identities should be included as part of socioemotional awareness for all educators. Specifically, opportunities for teachers to explore who they are and how they show up in this world, and opportunities for teachers to reflect on how these explorations inform their culture and identity are essential to counter and disrupt the perpetuation of colonizer/colonized narratives. These opportunities can increase how Latina teachers (and other teachers of Color) view teaching culture as a "social change strategy" (Lynn & Parker, 2006, p. 274).

The Latina teacher collaborators experienced a heightened awareness of their cultural roots in relation to living and teaching in predominantly non-Latinx spaces. The YAL texts were essential in establishing a means by which the teachers could examine the identity-journeys and intersectionalites of the identities of the Latina protagonists in America and their own unique experiences of being Latinas in the Deep South. "Research not only suggests that reading or listening to literature affects attitudes, but also that the active discussion of these values is just as important" (Aoki, 1993, p. 124). Curriculum specialists, staff development employees, and educators alike should be required to engage in cultural awareness and critical pedagogy endeavors, for example, in the form of critical book pláticas or book talks that include fiction and YAL, which provide more humanized and digestible counter-narratives from which to explore intersectionalities. Ideally, these book pláticas could be supported by and extended with explicit frameworks and critical perspectives such as CRT, LatCrit, Chicana/Latina Feminism, and culturally sustaining practices. Educators could, therefore, be immersed in diverse stories while also benefiting from explicit knowledge about how to approach these stories (e.g., from an asset-based versus deficit-based approach). These endeavors should be initially optional and primarily run by teachers, such as the collaborators of this study. These actions could also be initially supported by renewed partnerships with faculty or doctoral candidates from teacher education programs.

The Latina teachers featured in this book did not mention having had any means of mentorship or cultural support during their teacher education programs. While this was not a direct focus of the book, had they been exposed to culturally relevant and sustaining practices during their educator preparation or novice-teacher mentorship timeframe at their schools, their stories would have likely included more instances of critical consciousness, shared vulnerability, and collective empowerment. As Calderon et al. (2012) remind us, ". . . a shared vulnerability can be a source of cultural intuition that allows us to enter each other's lives . . . and become motivated to overcome pain, trauma, or grief; it engenders a solidarity that moves us toward a collective effort of healing, empowerment, and resistance" (p. 529). In addition, learning about ways to implement diverse critical perspectives in any curriculum, to include Latinx critical and realist fiction, "further presents the opportunity to discuss the ways Latina/o children [and other children of Color] can process institutional racism, patriarchal violence, and xenophobia" (Rodriguez, 2018, p. 63). When teachers of Color have an opportunity to explore their own lived experiences in a critical manner, they can in turn foster ways for their students to engage in similar processes.

## Where Do We Go from Here – Implications for Further Research

We tend to treat people the way that we perceive them, no matter how flawed or limiting our perceptions may be. The dangers of our (mis)perceptions, however, can be destructive, particularly racial microaggressions that cumulatively compound into harmful and distress-filled slights and assaults, which can then be internalized via the way in which an individual sees herself, her culture, and the world (Kohli & Solorzano, 2012). We must, therefore, continue to explore and share the multifaceted, nuanced, and ever-changing lived experiences of Latinx teachers with a loving gaze, since representation matters. Given that this book specifically centered three Latina teachers, a future study with more participants and participants of mixed gender identities would result in broader understanding and generalizability of the findings. In addition, a study that focuses specifically on intracultural understanding (e.g., by way of Latinx YAL) could also generate interesting findings. It is also imperative that future research about Latinx teachers include broader areas of intersectionalities and multiplicity, to include Afro-Latinx and queer Latinx perspectives (i.e., especially given the rise of YAL texts that specifically center such intersectionalities). Like this study, the use of critical YAL texts aimed at breaking from dominant Eurocentric experiences and text structures should remain as part of future research about Latinx teachers that center YAL texts. As García (2017) stressed:

> ... Latinx literature for youth functions as a counter-canon to both U.S. and Latin American tropes and norms. Today's Latinx authors for youth challenge the kind of internal and external racism, sexism, and classism that has rendered Latinxs invisible in U.S. and Latin American literature and society. (p. 117)

YAL texts should, therefore, continue to be used as a means to value, expand, and leverage the experiences of the characters and Latinx participants, particularly upon examining intracultural or intercultural experiences, since these texts often situate, "alternative perspectives of what it means to grow up as an American" (García, 2017, p. 116). Indeed, further research should also include examining intercultural experiences of Latinx teachers who teach predominantly Black students (and Black teachers who teach Latinx students). Doing so would promote culturally sustaining practices, problematize the normalization of student struggles, and explore how students of Color experience joy and love, thereby expanding upon critical consciousness. Let us not forget that, "In becoming a character, [we] can better understand motives and actions" (Aoki, 1993, p. 126).

This book allowed me to understand the benefits of using humanizing and critical methodological frameworks and approaches such as LatCrit, Chicana/Latina Feminism, muxerista portraiture, and testimonio. The findings would have likely been more personally unique to each individual Latina had the teachers written their own testimonios. Thus, future research will aim to include testimonios directly written by the Latinx participants. Doing so would encourage participants to "re-fram[e] [their] own family's history" (Sanchez & Ek, 2013, p. 182).

Additionally, further exploration using "critical qualitative inquiry" in the form of "imaginative methodology" like altered book tasks should be more predominantly centered as a primary means of data collection in research that aims to explore the lived experiences of Latinx teachers (Saavedra & Perez, 2017). Doing so would, "reinvent, reimagine research tools that allow a space for reconnection and foster interdependence instead of usurping knowledge and information from our participants" (Saavedra & Perez, 2017, p. 457). And while the original study included altered book tasks as a source of data collection, insufficient time was provided during the book pláticas to meaningfully center the altered books from which to conduct primary analysis. The inclusion of such creative and imaginative methodological approaches would allow the data collection to center the participant's experiences and the critical YAL texts featured, which portray Latinx characters who, "use creativity and imagination to challenge and transform the different forms of violence they experience in their lives" (Rodriguez, 2019, p. 9). In other words, the participants would use their creativity and imagination to help identify, challenge, and problematize the varying forms of racial violence they have experienced by way of the altered books. The inclusion of such imaginative methodologies and creative elements would facilitate a means to continue decolonizing ourselves (i.e., via the use of expansive frameworks and nontraditional, healing methodological approaches), thereby extending the current research on imaginative methodological approaches.

## Conclusion

The study upon which the book is based occurred during a tenuous time in history, within a historic presidential term and election, and against a major health pandemic that disproportionately affected communities of Color. Additionally, the time period right before, during, and shortly after the study was fraught with increasingly violent incidents of racial attacks on communities of Color (e.g., the horrific murders of George Floyd and Breonna Taylor, and immigrant children who were separated from their families in detention centers). This book seeks to explore the personal and schooling lived experiences of three Latina teachers in the Deep South. It aims to use three young adult literature (YAL) texts written by Latina authors to interrogate the identity-journeys and Latinx experiences of resilient protagonists in the United States and allow the Latina teachers to share convergent and/or divergent experiences. As Enciso (2017) reminds us, "Stories are central to the work of reimagining past, present, and future relations" (p. 30). Thus, I wanted to explore the complexities of being Latina in a geographic area bereft with a haunting civil rights history. I also aimed to use YAL that problematized a singular notion of an essentialized Latina, in addition to highlighting experiences of oppression and marginalization that culminated in increased Latina agency (i.e., via protagonists with self-affirming images of female Latinidad). I sought to explore and better understand what it means to be a Latina educator in the Deep South because of my own alienating experiences in a predominantly White institution of higher education. Thus, this book contributed to and extended the existing research by focusing on a population and geographic area with limited research. Additionally, the book explored the experiences of Latina teachers using YAL, a method that represented a gap in the current research.

The findings suggested that none of the three Latina teachers felt like genuine insiders, particularly at their schools of employment. Instead, they frequently shared stories about being otherized, not belonging, experiencing grief, and yearning for their cultural Homes and a sense of belongingness. All three expressed being grounded by their families and Latinx upbringing. This was evident via stories about strong mujeres, impactful mothers, and embodied ties to their Homes. Overall, the YAL texts were integral in guiding discussions about the lived experiences of the participants. From impressions about the text structures (e.g., poetry, traditional narrative, and mixed prose), to the character traits and experiences of the Latina protagonists, the YAL appeared to provide a foundational platform from which to discuss the collaborators' lived experiences. The YAL texts also appeared to result in a heightened awareness about the teachers' adolescent Latinx and Black students. These texts appeared to heighten the collaborators' own critical and hybrid consciousness by facilitating pláticas about what it means to explore Latinx identity. For example, Consuelo expressed not having previously considered how race and culture shape her life, while Lucero recounted how she hadn't thought about the ways that racial and cultural issues could become dire to adolescents, and Mercedes reflected on her limited friendships with Latinxs who only share her Puerto Rican identity.

Above all, the findings highlighted how the teachers mostly felt like outsiders, yet yearned to be accepted, valued, and celebrated for their unique Latina attributes. As Medina and Enciso (2002) highlighted, "many Latino/as born and raised in the U.S. ask where home is for them if 'home' is always experienced in both a U.S. context and in their parent's country of origin" (p. 40). While only one of the teachers was born in the contiguous United States, the notion of Home was expressed as a pained absence that was everpresent in the teachers' stories about their personal and schooling lived experiences.

Latina teachers in Alabama are adept at negotiating the in-between parts/gaps of nepantla – that is, the spaces of racial tension, confusion, and assimilation that are prevalent in non-Latinx spaces of the Deep South. Such negotiation and tolerance of living on the margins of cultural, racial, and/or social borders is where the Latina teachers in this study reside. Exposure, awareness, and cultivation of a nos/otras identity narrative and hybrid consciousness are essential to lessen the feeling of being "stuck between the cracks of home and other cultures ... [where] we experience dislocation, disorientation" (Anzaldúa, 2015, p. 81). Finding ways to connect to each other and explore the multifaceted and complex features that make our Latinidades beautifully complex and unique is a realistic endeavor that can be brought to fruition via "dreaming and artistic creativity" aimed at exploring "less structured thoughts, less rigid categorizations, and thinner boundaries" (Anzaldúa, 2015, p. 83). Such an exploration was enacted in this book by focusing on the findings of a study that centered the reading of Latinx YAL and responding to and sharing experiences via discussions and artistic artifact expressions at three book pláticas.

It is my hope that this book will broaden the understanding of Latina teachers as uniquely individual, with their own stories of Latinidad that converge and diverge in distinctly beautiful ways. It is my goal to continue exploring ways to advocate for equity and to counter and disrupt the perpetuation of colonizer/colonial narratives. Given the current sociopolitical climate and the ways in which the humanity of Latinxs (and other people of Color) have been stripped, questioned, and brutalized (particularly as a result of the Trump presidential term), it is of utmost importance to continue acknowledging and celebrating diverse humanity via research that centers teachers of Color. It is also my goal to continue using YAL texts written by authors of Color, to explore the lives of Latinx teachers and their intercultural and intracultural understandings. In doing so, I hope to also explore how they practice an "additive perspective" by way of "practices reflective of their bicultural realities" (García & Gaddes, 2012, p. 156), which would include imaginative methodological approaches such as the centralized use of altered books and/or testimonios written by the participants. Such explorations would, for example, continue to interrogate how Latinx teachers' connection with their environment and surroundings contributes to reimagining their self-identities (Anzaldúa, 2015). And isn't that what all of us most want ... to allow for the possibility to reimagine ourselves, ever-evolving, within the light of our own unique self-affirming attributes?

# Note

1    "... with a voice from the bottom of the abyss"

# REFERENCES

Acevedo, E. (2019). *The poet x*. Harper Collins.

ACLU Florida. (n.d.). *HB 1617/SB 1718 – Sweeping anti-immigrant bill*. https://www.aclufl.org/en/legislation/hb-1617sb-1718-sweeping-anti-immigrant-bill

Alamillo, L. (2007). Selecting Chicano children's literature in a bilingual classroom: Investigating issues of cultural authenticity and avoiding stereotypes. *Journal of the Association of Mexican American Educators, 1*(1), 26–32.

Anzaldúa, G. (1987). *Borderlands/la Frontera: The new mestiza* (4th ed.). Aunt Lute Books.

Anzaldúa, G. (1990). *Making face, making soul/hacienda caras: Creative and critical perspectives of feminists of color*. Aunt Lute Books.

Anzaldúa, G. (2002). Now let us shift . . . the path of conocimiento . . . inner work, public acts. In Gloria Anzaldúa & Analouise Keating (Eds.), *This bridge we call home: The radical visions for transformation* (pp. 540–578). Routledge.

Anzaldúa, G. (2015). *Light in the dark/Luz en lo oscuro: Rewriting identity, spirituality, reality* (A. Keating, Ed.). Duke University Press.

Aoki, E. M. (1993). Turning the page: Asian Pacific American children's literature. In V. J. Harris (Ed.), *Teaching multicultural literature in grades k-8* (pp. 109–135). Christopher-Gordon Publishers, Inc.

Bishop, R. S. (1990). Mirrors, windows, and sliding glass doors. *Perspectives: Choosing and using books for the classroom, 6*(3).

Brabeck, K. (2003). Testimonio: A strategy for collective resistance, cultural survival and building solidarity. *Feminism & Psychology, 12*(2), 252–258.

Burciaga, R., & Tavares, A. (2006). Our pedagogy of sisterhood: A testimonio. In D. Delgado Bernal, C. A. Elenes, F. E. Godinez, & S. Villenas (Eds.), *Chicana/Latina feminist pedagogies and epistemologies of everyday life: Educatión en la familia, comunidad y escuela* (pp. 133–142). State University of New York Press.

Bustos Flores, B., Riojas Clark, E., Claeys, L., & Villarreal, A. (2007). Academy for teacher excellence: Recruiting, preparing, and retaining Latino teachers through learning communities. *Teacher Education Quarterly, 34*(4), 53–69.

Cai, M. (2002). Multicultural literature for children and young adults: Reflections on critical issues. Greenwood Press.

Calderon, D., Delgado Bernal, D., Velez, V. N., Perez Huber, L., & Malagon, M. (2012). A Chicana feminist epistemology revisited: Cultivating ideas a generation later. *Harvard Educational Review, 82*(4), 513–539.

Cisneros, S. (1984). *The house on mango street.* Vintage Contemporaries.

Clandinin, D. J., & Connelly, F. M. (2000). *Narrative inquiry: Experience and story in qualitative research.* Jossey-Bass.

Colomer, S. E. (2014). Latina Spanish high school teachers' negotiation of capital in new Latino communities. *Bilingual Research Journal, 37*(3), 349–365.

Creswell, J. W., & Poth, C. N. (2018). *Qualitative inquiry and research design* (4th ed.). Sage Publications, Inc.

De Brey, C., Musu, L., McFarland, J., Wilkinson-Flicker, S., Diliberti, M., Zhang, A., Branstetter, C., & Wang, X. (2019). *Status and trends in the education or racial and ethnic groups 2018* (NCES Publication No. 2019–032). U.S. Department of Education. Washington, D.C.: National Center for Educational Statistics. http://nces.ed.gov/pubsearch/

Delgado Bernal, D. (1998). Using a Chicana feminist epistemology in educational research. *Harvard Educational Review, 68*(4), 555–583.

Delgado Bernal, D., Burciaga, R., & Flores Carmona, J. (2012). Chicana/Latina testimonios: Mapping the methodological, pedagogical, and political. *Equity & Excellence in Education, 45*(3), 363–372.

Delgado Bernal, D. (2016). Cultural intuition: Then, now, and into the future. *Center for Critical Race Studies at UCLA: Research Briefs, 1,* 1–4.

Delgado, R. (1989). Storytelling for oppositionists: A plea for narrative. *Michigan Law Review, 87*(8), 2411–2441.

Delgado, R. (1995). *Critical race theory: The cutting edge.* Temple University Press.

Delgado, R., & Stefancic, J. (2001). *Critical race theory: An introduction.* New York University Press.

Easton-Brooks, D. (2013). Ethnic matching in urban schools. In R. Milner & K. Lomotey (Eds.), *Handbook of urban education* (pp. 97–113). Routledge.

Emerson, R. M., Fretz, R. I., & Shaw, L. L. (2011). *Writing ethnographic fieldnotes* (2nd ed.). The University of Chicago Press.

Enciso, P. (2017). Stories lost and found: Mobilizing imagination in literacy research and practice. *Literacy Research: Theory, Method, and Practice, 66,* 29–52.

Espino, M. M., Muñoz, S. M., & Marquez Kiyama, J. (2010). Transitioning from doctoral study to the academy: Theorizing trenzas of identity for Latina sister scholars. *Qualitative Inquiry, 16*(10), 804–818.

Faulk, K. (2019, March 7). Court rules Gardendale can't form school system, finds racial motives; city to appeal. *Birmingham Real-Time News.* https://www.al.com/news/birming ham/2018/02/federal_appeals_court_rules_ga.html

Fierros, C. O., & Delgado Bernal, D. (2016). Vamos a platicar: The contours of pláticas as Chicana/Latina feminist methodology. *Chicana/Latina Studies, 15*(2), 98–121.

Flores, A. I. (2017a). Muxerista portraiture: Portraiture with a Chicana/Latina feminist sensibility. *Center for Critical Race Studies at UCLA: Research Briefs, 7,* 1–4.

Flores, A. I. (2017b). The muxerista portraitist: Engaging portraiture and Chicana feminist theories in qualitative research. *Chicana/Latina Studies, 17*(1), 60–93.

Flores, J., & García, S. (2009). Latina testimonios: A reflexive, critical analysis of a 'Latina space' at a predominantly White campus. *Race Ethnicity and Education, 12*(2), 155–172.

Flores Carmona, J., & Luciano, A. M. (2014). A student-teacher testimonio: Reflexivity, empathy, and pedagogy. *Counterpoints – Crafting Critical Stories: Toward Pedagogies and Methodologies of Collaboration, Inclusion, and Voice, 449,* 75–92.

Flores, G. M. (2011). Racialized tokens: Latina teachers negotiating, surviving and thriving in a White woman's profession. *Qualitative Sociology, 34,* 313–335.

Flores, T. T., Batista-Morales, N., & Salmerón, C. (2019). Authoring future identities: Latina girls reading and writing the university. *Multicultural Perspectives, 21*(3), 139–147.

García, A., & Gaddes, A. (2012) Weaving language and culture: Latina adolescent writers in an after-school writing project. *Reading & Writing Quarterly, 28*(2), 143–163.

García, M. J. (2018). En(countering) YA: Young lords, shadowshapers, and the longings and possibilities of Latinx young adult literature. *Latino Studies, 16,* 230–249.

García, M. J. (2017). Side by side: At the intersections of Latinx studies and ChYALit. *The Lion and the Unicorn, 41,* 113–122.

Ginwright, S. (2018, May 31). *The future of healing: Shifting from trauma informed care to healing centered engagement.* Medium. https://ginwright.medium.com/the-future-of-healing-shift ing-from-trauma-informed-care-to-healing-centered-engagement-634f557ce69c#

Godinez, F. E. (2006). Haciendo que hacer: Braiding cultural knowledge into educational practices and policies. In D. Delgado Bernal, C. A. Elenes, F. E. Godinez, & S. Villenas (Eds.), *Chicana/Latina education in everyday life: Feminista perspectives on pedagogy and epistemology* (pp. 25–38). State University of New York.

Gomez, M. L. (2010). Talking about ourselves, talking about our mothers: Latina prospective teachers narrate their life experiences. *Urban Review, 42*(2), 81–101.

Gomez, M. L., & Rodriguez, T. L. (2011). Imagining the knowledge, strengths, and skills of a Latina prospective teacher. *Teacher Education, 38*(1), 127–146.

González, N., Moll, L. C., & Amanti, C. (2005). *Funds of knowledge: Theorizing practices in households, communities and classrooms.* Erlbaum.

Goodall, H. L., Jr. (2000). *Writing the new ethnography.* AltaMira Press.

Gordon, J. (2005). Inadvertent complicity: Colorblindness in teacher education. *Educational Studies, 38*(2), 135–153.

Guggenheim, D. (Director). (2006). *An inconvenient truth* [Film]. Lawrence Bender Productions; Participant Productions.

Gutierrez, K., Baquedano-Lopez, P., & Tejeda, C. (1999). Rethinking diversity: Hybridity and hybrid language practices in the third space. *Mind, Culture, and Activity, 6,* 283–303.

Hayn, J. A., Kaplan, J. S., & Nolen, A. (2011). Young adult literature research in the 21st century. *Theory Into Practice, 50,* 176–181.

Hernandez, C. D. (2019). *Knitting the fog.* Feminist Press.

Hernandez-Truyol, B. (1997). Borders (en)gendered: Normativities, Latinas and a LatCrit paradigm. *New York University Law Review, 72,* 882–927.

Hughes-Hassell, S. (2013). Multicultural young adult literature as a form of counter-storytelling. *Library Quarterly: Information, Community, Policy, 83*(3), 212–228.

Ingersoll, R. M. (2012). Beginning teacher induction: What the data tell us. *Phi Delta Kappan.* Education Week. https://www.edweek.org/ew/articles/2012/05/16/kappan_ingersoll.h31.html

Ingersoll, R. M., May, H., & Collins, G. (2019). Recruitment, employment, retention and the minority teacher shortage. *Education Policy Analysis Archives, 27*(37), 1–42.

Irizarry, J. G., & Donaldson, M. L. (2012). Teach for America: The Latinization of U.S. schools and the critical shortage of Latina/o teachers. *American Educational Research Journal, 49*(1), 155–194.

Kayi-Aydar, H. (2018). "If Carmen can analyze Shakespeare, everybody can": Positions, conflicts, and negotiations in the narratives of Latina pre-service teachers. *Journal of Language, Identity & Education, 17*(2), 118–130.

Kiyama, J. M. (2018). "We're serious about our education": A collective testimonio from college-going Latinas to college personnel. *Journal of Hispanic Higher Education, 17*(4), 415–429.

Kohli, R. (2018). Behind school doors: The impact of hostile racial climates on urban teachers of color. *Urban Education, 53*(3), 307–333.

Kohli, R. (2014). Unpacking internalized racism: Teachers of color striving for racially just classrooms. *Race Ethnicity and Education, 17*(3), 367–387.

Kohli, R., & Solorzano, D. (2012). Teachers, please learn our names!: Racial microaggressions and the K-12 classroom. *Race Ethnicity and Education, 15*(4), 1–22.

Korte, G., & Gomez, A. (2018, May 16). *Trump ramps rhetoric on undocumented immigrant. 'These aren't people. These are animal.'* USA Today. https://www.usatoday.com/story/news/politics/2018/05/16/trump-immigrants-animals-mexico-democrats-sanctuary-cities/617252002/

Krogstad, J. M. (2020, July 10). *Hispanics have accounted for more than half of total U.S. population growth since 2010.* Pew Research Center: FactTank News in the Numbers. https://www.pewresearch.org/fact-tank/2020/07/10/hispanics-have-accounted-for-more-than-half-of-total-u-s-population-growth-since-2010/

Krogstad, J. M. (2016, September 8). *Key facts about how the U.S. Hispanic population is changing.* Pew Research Center: FactTank News in the Numbers. https://www.pewresearch.org/fact-tank/2016/09/08/key-facts-about-how-the-u-s-hispanic-population-is-changing/

Ladson-Billings, G. (2000). Racialized discourses and ethnic epistemologies. In N. K. Denzin & Y. S. Lincoln (Eds.), *Handbook of qualitative research*, 2nd ed., Sage.

Lawrence-Lightfoot, S. (1994). *I've known rivers: Lives of loss and liberation.* Addison-Wesley Publishing Company.

Lawrence-Lightfoot, S., & Davis, J. H. (1997). *The art and science of portraiture.* Jossey-Bass Publishers.

Lawrence-Lightfoot, S. (2005). Reflections on portraiture: A dialogue between art and science. *Qualitative Inquiry, 11*(1), 3–15.

Lynn, M., & Parker, L. (2006). Critical race studies in education: Examining a decade of research on U.S. school. *The Urban Review, 38*(4), 257–290.

Martinez, V. L. (2017). Testimonio praxis in educational spaces: Lessons from mujeres in the field. *Association of Mexican American Educators, 11*(1), 38–53.

Martinez-Roldan, C. M., & Quinones, S. (2016). Resisting erasure and developing networks of solidarity: Testimonios of two Puerto Rican scholars in the academy. *Journal of Language, Identity & Education, 15*(3), 151–164.

Matsuda, M. (1991). Voices of America: Accent, antidiscrimination law, and a jurisprudence for the last reconstruction. *Yale Law Journal, 100*, 1329–1407.

Medina, Y. (2009). Art education programs: Empowering social change. *Perspectives on Urban Education*, 58–61.

Medina, C., & Enciso, P. (2002). "Some words are messengers/hay palabras mensajeras": Interpreting sociopolitical themes in Latino/o children's literature. *New Advocate, 15*(1), 35–47.

Menchu, R. (1984). *I, Rigoberta Menchu: An Indian woman in Guatemala.* E. Burgos-Debray (Ed.) & (A. Wright, Trans.). Verso.

Mijs, J. (2016). The unfulfilled promise of meritocracy: Three lessons and their implications for justice in education. *Social Justice Research, 29*, 14–34.

Montoya, M. E. (1994). *Mascaras, trenzas, y greñas:* Un/masking the self while un/braiding Latina stories and legal discourse. *Harvard Women's Law Journal, 17*(1), 185–220.

Monzó, L. D. (2015). Ethnography in charting paths toward personal and social liberation: Using my Latina cultural intuition. *International Journal of Qualitative Education, 28*(4), 373–393.

Moraga, C., & Anzaldúa, G. (1983). *This bridge called my back: Writings by radical women of color.* Kitchen Table: Women of Color Press.

National Center for Education Statistics (n.d.). *Common core of data/Search for public school districts.* Retrieved October 20, 2020. https://nces.ed.gov/ccd/districtsearch/index.asp

National Council of La Raza. (n.d.). *Alabama state fact sheet.* https://guides.library.uab.edu/ld.php?content_id=44204490

Noe-Bustamante, L., Mora, L., & Lopez, M. H. (2020). *About one-in-four U.S. Hispanics have heard of Latinx, but just 3% use it.* Pew Research Center. https://www.pewresearch.org/hispanic/2020/08/11/about-one-in-four-u-s-hispanics-have-heard-of-Latinx-but-just-3-use-it/

Ocasio, K. M. (2014). Nuestro Camino: A review of literature surrounding the Latino teacher pipeline. *Journal of Latinos & Education, 13*(4), 244–261.

Ochoa, L. (2016). Documenting the undocumented: Testimonios as humanizing pedagogy. *Association of Mexican American Educators, 10*(2), 49–64.

Osorio, S. L. (2018). Border stories: Using critical race and Latino critical theories to understand the experiences of Latino/a children. *Race Ethnicity and Education, 21*(1), 92–104.

Perez-Huber, L. (2010). Using Latina/o critical race theory (LatCrit) and racist nativism to explore intersectionality in the educational experiences of undocumented Chicana college students. *Educational Foundations, 24*(1–2), 77–96.

Pink, S., & Morgan, J. (2013). Short-term ethnography and intense routes to knowing. *Symbolic Interaction, 36*, 351–361.

Pour-Khorshid, F. (2018). Cultivating sacred spaces: A racial affinity group approach to support critical educators of color. *Teaching Education, 29*(4), 318–329.

Reyes, K. B., & Curry Rodriguez, J. E. (2012). Testimonio: Origins, terms, and resources. *Equity & Excellence in Education, 45*(3), 525–538.

Robinson, J., Paccione, A., & Rodriguez, F. (2003). A place where people care: A case study of recruitment and retention of minority-group teachers. *Equity & Excellence in Education, 36*, 202–212.

Rodriguez, S. A. (2019). Conocimiento narratives: Creative acts and healing in Latinx children's and young adult literature. *Children's Literature, 47*, 9–29.

Rodriguez, S. A. (2018). School fights: Resisting Oppression in the classroom in Gloria Velasquez's Latina/o young adult novel – Juanita fights the board. *Children's Literature in Education, 49*, 61–72.

Rosenblatt, L. (1978). *The reader, the text and the poem: The transactional theory of the literary work.* Southern Illinois University Press.

Saavedra, C. M., & Perez, M. S. (2012). Chicana and Black feminisms:Testimonios of theory, identity, and multiculturalism. *Equity & Excellence in Education, 45*(3), 430–443.

Saavedra, C. M., & Perez, M. S. (2017). Chicana/Latina feminist critical qualitative inquiry: Meditations on global solidarity, spirituatlity, and the land. *International Review of Qualitative Research, 10*(4), 450–467.

Saldaña, J. (2016). *The coding manual for qualitative researchers* (3rd ed.). Sage Publications Ltd.

Sanchez, P., & Ek, L. D. (2013). Cultivando la siguiente generacion: Future directions in Chicana/Latina feminist pedagogies. *Journal of Latino/Latin American Studies, 5*(3), 181–187.

Sanchez, E. L. (2017). *I am not your perfect Mexican daughter.* Alfred A. Knopf.

Sciurba, K. (2014). Texts as mirrors, texts as windows: Black adolescent boys and the complexities of textual relevance. *Journal of Adolescent & Adult Literacy, 58*(4), 308–316.

Scott, E. (2019, October 2). *Trump's most insulting – and violent – language is often reserved for immigrants. The Washington Post.* https://www.washingtonpost.com/politics/2019/10/02/trumps-most-insulting-violent-language-is-often-reserved-immigrants/

Sheets, C. (2017, March 24). Alabama's 2011 anti-immigrant law H.B. 56 still on books, gets new life under Trump. *AL.com.* https://www.al.com/news/birmingham/index.ssf/2017/03/hb_56_alabamas_2011_anti-immig.html

Solorzano, D. G., & Delgado Bernal, D. (2001). Examining transformational resistance through a critical race and LatCrit theory framework: Chicana and Chicano students in an urban context. *Urban Education, 36*(3), 308–342.

Solorzano, D. G., & Yosso, T. J. (2001). Critical race and LatCrit theory and method: Counter-storytelling. *Qualitative Studies in Education, 14*(4), 471–495.

Sosa-Provencio, M. A., Sheahan, A., Fuentes, R., Muniz, S., & Vivas, R. E. P. (2019). Reclaiming ourselves through testimonio pedagogy: Reflections on a curriculum design lab in teacher education. *Race Ethnicity and Education, 22*(2), 211–230.

Soto Huerta, M. E. (2019). Living and co-constructing liminal pathways for Latinx preservice teachers. *Cultural Studies – Critical Methodologies, 19*(3), 222–230.

Southern Poverty Law Center (SPLC). (2021, June, 25). *A cruel legacy: Alabama anti-immigrant law remembered.* https://www.splcenter.org/news/2021/06/25/cruel-legacy-alabama-anti-immigrant-law-remembered.

Spradley, J. P. (2016). *The ethnographic interview.* Waveland Press, Inc. (Original work published 1979)

Stepler, R., & Lopez, M. H. (2016). *U.S. Latino population growth and dispersion has slowed since onset of the great recession.* Pew Research Center. https://www.pewresearch.org/hispanic/2016/09/08/1-u-s-hispanic-population-dispersion-before-and-after-the-onset-of-the-great-recession/

Tedlock, B. (1991). From participant observation to the observation of participation: The emergence of narrative ethnography. *Journal of Anthropological Research, 47*(1), 69–94.

The Latina Feminist Group. (2001). *Telling to live: Latina feminist testimonios.* Duke University Press.

UCLA Library's Center for Oral History Research. (2015). *Family history sample outline and questions.* https://oralhistory.library.ucla.edu/pages/family_history

UnidosUS (formerly The National Council of La Raza). (2016). *Alabama State Fact Sheet.* https://unidosus.org/publications/890-alabama-state-fact-sheet/

United States Census Bureau. (n.d.). *Quick facts – Jefferson County, Alabama.* Retrieved October 20, 2020. https://www.census.gov/quickfacts/jeffersoncountyalabama

Valdes, F. (1997). Under construction: LatCrit consciousness, community, and theory. *California Law Review, 85*(5), 1089–1141.

Wolk, S. (2009). Reading for a better world: Teaching for social responsibility with young adult literature. *Journal of Adolescent & Adult Literacy, 52*(8), 664–673.

Young Adult Library Services Association. (2008). *The value of young adult literature.* http://www.ala.org/yalsa/guidelines/whitepapers/yalit

# APPENDIX A

## TEXT COVERS AND SUMMARIES OF BOOKS USED IN ORIGINAL STUDY

*Knitting the Fog*, by Claudia D. Hernandez, tells the story of Claudia, who lives in Guatemala with her family until her mother flees to the United States to get away from her abusive father when she's seven years old. Claudia and her two older sisters are temporarily raised by their great aunt and grandmother until they move to Los Angeles to join her mother when Claudia is ten years old. Upon moving to a predominantly Mexican neighborhood, Claudia faces challenges assimilating, learning English, and balancing the parts of herself that make her unique.

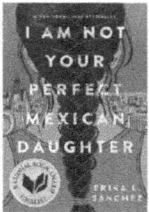

*I am Not Your Perfect Mexican Daughter*, by Erika L. Sanchez, tells the story of Julia, who struggles to fulfill her parents' expectations of a Mexican daughter after her older sister tragically dies. The setting is Chicago, where Julia is in high school and falls in love for the first time. Throughout the novel, Julia attempts to balance managing her family's grief (in particular, her mother) and learning secrets about her sister, all of which lead to emotional instability that culminate in Julia being sent to visit her family in Mexico. Ultimately, Julia explores her identity and learns about family secrets that help her better understand her mother.

*The Poet* X, by Elizabeth Acevedo, is about Xiomara, who is Dominican and lives in Harlem. She doesn't fit the traditional role of a feminine Latina daughter and struggles to be understood by her parents, especially her mother. Written in verse/poems, Xiomara explores her feelings of cultural isolation and resilient strength via her poetry slam poems.

# APPENDIX B

## PRE/POST-QUESTIONNAIRE QUESTIONS FROM ORIGINAL STUDY

### Pre-questionnaire Questions

1. Name:
2. Age:
3. How do you identify culturally?
4. What language(s) are you fluent in?
5. How beneficial is it for you to be familiar with your Latino/a students' cultural backgrounds?

   Not Beneficial        Somewhat Beneficial    Very Beneficial
   
   1    2    3    4    5    6    7    8    9    10

6. If you answered two or above on question five, identify three reasons why it is beneficial for you as a teacher to understand your Latino/a students' cultural backgrounds.

   1.
   2.
   3.

7. How interested are you in having discussions with Latina teachers (of <u>different</u> cultural background than you) about your culture/Latinidad?

| Not Interested | | | | Somewhat Interested | | | | Very Interested | |
|---|---|---|---|---|---|---|---|---|---|
| 1 | 2 | 3 | 4 | 5 | 6 | 7 | 8 | 9 | 10 |

8. How comfortable do you feel having discussions with other Latinas (of <u>different</u> cultural background than you) about your culture/Latinidad?

| Not Interested | | | | Somewhat Interested | | | | Very Interested | |
|---|---|---|---|---|---|---|---|---|---|
| 1 | 2 | 3 | 4 | 5 | 6 | 7 | 8 | 9 | 10 |

9. How interested are you in having discussions with Latina teachers (of the <u>same</u> cultural background as you) about your culture/Latinidad?

| Not Interested | | | | Somewhat Interested | | | | Very Interested | |
|---|---|---|---|---|---|---|---|---|---|
| 1 | 2 | 3 | 4 | 5 | 6 | 7 | 8 | 9 | 10 |

10. How comfortable do you feel having discussions with other Latinas (of the <u>same</u> cultural background as you) about your culture/Latinidad?

| Not Interested | | | | Somewhat Interested | | | Very Interested | |
|---|---|---|---|---|---|---|---|---|
| 1 | 2 | 3 | 4 | 5 | 6 | 7 | 8 | 9 | 10 |

11. What do you hope to gain from participating in this study?

## Post-questionnaire Questions

1. How do you identify culturally?
2. What language(s) are you fluent in?
3. How beneficial is it for you to be familiar with your Latino/a students' cultural backgrounds?

| Not Beneficial | | | | Somewhat Beneficial | | | | Very Beneficial | |
|---|---|---|---|---|---|---|---|---|---|
| 1 | 2 | 3 | 4 | 5 | 6 | 7 | 8 | 9 | 10 |

4. If you answered two or above on question three, identify three reasons why it is beneficial for you as a teacher to understand your Latino/a students' cultural backgrounds.

1.
2.
3.

5. How interested are you in having discussions with Latina teachers (of <u>different</u> cultural background than you) about your culture/Latinidad?

| Not Interested | | | | Somewhat Interested | | | | Very Interested | |
|---|---|---|---|---|---|---|---|---|---|
| 1 | 2 | 3 | 4 | 5 | 6 | 7 | 8 | 9 | 10 |

6. How comfortable do you feel having discussions with other Latinas (of <u>different</u> cultural background than you) about your culture/Latinidad?

| Not Interested | | | | Somewhat Interested | | | | Very Interested | |
|---|---|---|---|---|---|---|---|---|---|
| 1 | 2 | 3 | 4 | 5 | 6 | 7 | 8 | 9 | 10 |

7. How interested are you in having discussions with Latina teachers (of the <u>same</u> cultural background as you) about your culture/Latinidad?

| Not Interested | | | | Somewhat Interested | | | | Very Interested | |
|---|---|---|---|---|---|---|---|---|---|
| 1 | 2 | 3 | 4 | 5 | 6 | 7 | 8 | 9 | 10 |

8. How comfortable do you feel having discussions with other Latinas (of the <u>same</u> cultural background as you) about your culture/Latinidad?

| Not Interested | | | | Somewhat Interested | | | | Very Interested | |
|---|---|---|---|---|---|---|---|---|---|
| 1 | 2 | 3 | 4 | 5 | 6 | 7 | 8 | 9 | 10 |

9. Briefly describe what you feel you gained from participating in this study.
10. What would you keep the same about the study?
11. What would you change about the study?

# APPENDIX C

## INTRODUCTORY, SECOND, AND THIRD INTERVIEW QUESTIONS FROM ORIGINAL STUDY

| Item: | **Introductory Interview Questions** |
|---|---|

Introduction:

Thank you for taking the time to speak with me today. We are going to start with a 10–15-minute questionnaire I'd like for you to fill out. Then we will begin the interview.

As I noted earlier in the informed consent acknowledgement statement, participation in this study is voluntary. At any point in the research process if you would like to discontinue participation, you are welcome to do so. There are no expected risks to this study.

In addition, I want to remind you that your participation in this study will be confidential. In my dissertation and any published reports, there will be no information included that will make it possible to identify you. Research records will be stored securely, and I will be the only researcher to have access to the records.

Do you have any questions before you start the questionnaire and then we move on to the interview questions?

Please take a few minutes to answer the Introductory Interview Questionnaire.

Now we will begin the interview. Keep in mind that I may ask a followup question to your responses. These questions were adapted from UCLA's *Family History Sample Outline and Questions* (2015).

**A. Parents and Family – This first section focuses on general questions about your family and how you came to live in Alabama.**

1. Tell me about your family background.
2. Tell me about your parents or guardians. What role do they or have they played in your life?
3. What are some of your favorite childhood memories with your family? Why are they memorable to you?
4. Could you tell me about your family's home country?
5. Describe how your family ended up in Alabama.

**B. School – This second section focuses on your K-12 schooling experiences.**

6. What type of schools did you attend when you were younger?
7. Did you have any memorable teachers? Can you tell me about an interaction with this teacher that really struck out to you?
8. What impact do you feel your teachers had on you, if any?
9. Can you tell me about an interaction that really struck out to you?
10. What were your plans when you finished school?
11. What did your parents or family think of your plans?

**C. Adulthood and Identity – We're moving to the third section now; this section will be about your cultural experiences as an adult.**

12. How do you identify racially/culturally? Has this identification changed over time? How so? Is your cultural identity important to you? Why/why not?
13. Have you ever felt like you have two or more identities (e.g., Mexican and American)? Describe this experience.
14. Have you ever experienced or witnessed racial or cultural discrimination? If so, how did this experience affect you?
15. Explain what it means to be an outsider.
16. Can you tell me about a time when you felt like an outsider?
17. Explain what it means to be an insider.
18. Can you tell me about a time when you felt like an insider?

**D. Educator Experiences – This is the last section for today and it focuses on your experiences as a teacher.**

19. Why did you decide to become a teacher?
20. How did or has your culture influenced you as a teacher?
21. What experiences as a teacher have made you feel most like yourself?
22. What experiences as a teacher have made you feel less accepted?
23. Is there anything else that you would like to add?

Item:                       **Second Interview Questions**

Introduction:

Thank you so much for agreeing to do a followup interview. We are going to start with a 10–15-minute questionnaire I'd like for you to fill out. This questionnaire is similar to the questionnaire filled out at the first introductory interview.

Questions:

1. Based on what we talked about in the initial interview, I would greatly appreciate if you could elaborate on the following:
   o challenges and rewards of being a Latina teacher
   o support systems for Latina teachers
   o opportunities for ongoing professional development for Latina teachers
   o advice and recommendations for other Latinas contemplating a career in teaching in the Deep South

2. After the first interview or last focus group session, did any topics arise that kept you thinking after the interview or focus group ended? If so, could you elaborate on those?

3. Is there anything else that you would like to add?

Item:                    **Third Interview Questions**

Introduction:

Thank you so much for agreeing to do this final interview. Now that I have begun analyzing the responses from the first two interviews and the three focus groups, I would like to briefly review some initial findings and emerging themes, so you can provide feedback, ask questions, and clarify some responses. I would also like to share some preliminary descriptions that I have written about your altered book and the experiences you have shared throughout the study, in addition to some quotes that I may use for scholarly publications.

Questions:

1. After the first two interviews and the three focus group sessions, did any topics arise that kept you thinking after the interviews or focus group sessions ended? If so, could you elaborate on those?
2. I'd like to share a summary of my findings thus far. Please let me know if I accurately depicted your sentiments and/or what revisions you recommend. Do you have revisions and/or feedback?
3. I would now like to share some descriptions I have written about your altered book and the experiences you have shared during the study. Please read them, make any notations or edits, and let me know if I accurately depicted your sentiments and/or what revisions you recommend. Do you have revisions and/or feedback?
4. Now I would like to share some of your quotes from the interviews and focus group sessions. Please read them, make any notations or edits, and let me know if I accurately depicted your sentiments and/or what revisions you recommend. Do you have revisions and/or feedback?

5. Is there anything else that you would like to add?

# APPENDIX D

## BOOK PLÁTICA QUESTIONS FROM ORIGINAL STUDY

1. With which character do you most relate to in the book? Can you describe why?
2. Can you recall at least one part of the book that really spoke to you?
3. Describe why this part spoke to you.
4. Tell me about any personal memories that the book reminded you of.
5. Were you able to see yourself reflected in the book? Describe how.
6. What type of hardships did you notice in the book? Can you describe your reaction to these? How did they make you feel?
7. What challenges does the main character face trying to assimilate in the book? Did you relate to these challenges? If so, describe how.
8. How are family dynamics described or included in the book? Can you describe any connections you made to family dynamics in the book?
9. What do you remember about how the main characters' male and female relatives are portrayed in the book? Can you relate to these portrayals? If so, describe how.
10. Can you describe your greatest take-away from the book?

# APPENDIX E

# ALTERED BOOK PROMPTS FROM THE ORIGINAL STUDY

Altered Book Prompt for Book Platica One:

Use one individual page or an entire spread of the book to respond to the following paired questions by using images, words, drawings, and/or found objects:

1. How does the main character appear to others on the outside?
2. What do you know about the main character's inner-self?
3. If time permits, how do you appear to others on the outside?
4. If time permits, describe your inner-self.
5. Written Exit Slip –What advice would you offer the main character based on your personal experiences? Briefly reflect on today's session – what are your take-aways; what is your artist's statement about your altered book creation?

Altered Book Prompt for Book Platica Two:

Use one individual page or an entire spread of the book to respond to the following paired questions by using images, words, drawings, and/or found objects:

1. What does the main character most want?

2. What type of conflict do these desires create?
3. If time permits, what do you want most?
4. If time permits, what conflicts arise from your desires?
5. Written Exit Slip –What advice would you offer the main character based on your personal experiences? Briefly reflect on today's session – what are your take-aways; what is your artist's statement about your altered book creation?

Altered Book Prompt for Book Platica Three:

Use one individual page or an entire spread of the book to respond to the following questions by using images, words, drawings, and/or found objects:

1. Use the superhero stencil or draw your own and indicate the following information about the main character –
   a. If she were a superhero, what would be her name?
   b. Depict her superpowers.
   c. Identify and display descriptive words to represent her powers.

2. Use the superhero stencil or draw your own and indicate the following information about you –
   a. If you were a superhero, what would be your name?
   b. Depict your superpowers.
   c. Identify and display descriptive words to represent your powers.

3. Written Exit Slip –What advice would you offer the main character based on your personal experiences? Briefly reflect on today's session – what are your take-aways; what is your artist's statement about your altered book creation?

# GLOSSARY

*Color-neutrality* Sometimes referred to as "color-blindness," color-neutrality refers to a refusal or resistance to see skin color. "This resistance is learned and nurtured to protect the status quo, which privileges White people and occurs on both the individual and systemic levels" (Gordon, 2005, p. 139).

*Counter-narratives and counter-stories* Fiction or nonfiction writing or texts that aim to "cast doubt on the validity of accepted" normalized accounts or "myths, especially ones held by the majority" (Delgado & Stefanic, 2001, p. 144).

*Critical Race Theory (CRT)* A legal movement and theoretical framework "that seeks to transform the relationship among race, racism, and power" (Delgado & Stefanic, 2001, p. 144). Within education, CRT seeks to problematize and center how race and racism intersect with other forms of subordination by challenging dominant ideologies, committing to social justice, centering experiential knowledge, and providing a "transdisciplinary perspective" (Solorzano & Yosso, 2001, p. 473).

*Cultural intuition* A unique perspective that "draws from personal experience, collective experience, professional experience, communal memory, existing literature, and the research process itself" (Delgado Bernal, 2016, p. 1).

*Latino/a Critical Race Theory (LatCrit)* An extension of CRT that central-izes issues and areas of intersectionality that are specific to Latinxs such as immigration, citizenship, language, and hybrid identities (Delgado & Stefanic, 2001).

*Latinx(s)* While many individuals from the pan-ethnic diaspora with Spanish and Latin American roots refer to themselves as "Hispanic," I have chosen to use the term "Latinx" in this study, given that the term "Hispanic" has origins from the U.S. Government (i.e., a government that has historically oppressed communities of Color) (Noe-Bustamante, Mora, & Lopez, 2020). I also use "Latinx" to be inclusive of gender fluidity. Thus, in this study, "Latinx" (and the plural, "Latinxs") refers to individuals that have been traditionally referred to as "Latino/a" or "Hispanic," yet is used to convey gender inclusivity and challenge the gender binary that comprises the Spanish language. I also use the term "Latina" when referencing the participants, since they frequently used this term to self-identify themselves.

*Latinidad* Represents the essence of being a Latinx individual or being from a Latinx community/culture/country.

*Meritocracy* Success in work and school can be attributed to talent, hard work, and "individual worthiness" (Delgado & Stefanic, 2001, p. 150). The concept of meritocracy, however, ignores the "inequalities of opportunity" prevalent in society, and how the definition of merit "serve[s] some people, while disadvan-taging others" that do not mirror the White status-quo in society (Mijs, 2016, pp. 15–16).

*Microaggression(s)* Routine or "stunning small encounter[s]" and racial assaults that are targeted toward people of Color, sometimes "unnoticed by members of the majority race" (Delgado & Stefanic, 2001, p. 151; Kohli, 2018).

*Testimonio(s)* Testimonies or personal narratives that incorporate "political, social, historical, and cultural histories that accompany one's life experiences as a means to bring about change through consciousness-raising" (Delgado Bernal et al., 2012, p. 364). Testimonios can be written by an outsider or by oneself, and can be presented as a story, poem, memoir, oral history, or other formats – what remains true is that it is "intentional and political" (Reyes & Curry Rodriguez, 2012, p. 525).

# Critical Studies of LATINXS in the Americas

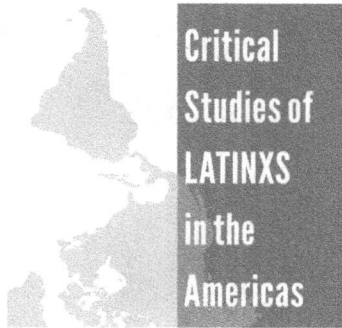

## Yolanda Medina and Margarita Machado-Casas
### GENERAL EDITORS

Critical Studies of Latinxs in the Americas is a provocative interdisciplinary series that offers a critical space for reflection and questioning what it means to be Latinxs living in the Americas in twenty-first century social, cultural, economic, and political arenas. The series looks forward to extending the dialogue to include the North and South Western hemispheric relations that are prevalent in the field of global studies.

Topics that explore and advance research and scholarship on contemporary topics and issues related with processes of racialization, economic exploitation, health, education, transnationalism, immigration, gendered and sexual identities, and disabilities that are not commonly highlighted in the current Latinx Studies literature as well as the multitude of socio, cultural, economic, and political progress among the Latinxs in the Americas are welcome.

To receive more information about CSLA, please contact:

Yolanda Medina (ymedina@bmcc.cuny.edu) &
Margarita Machado-Casas (mmachadocasas@sdsu.edu)

To order other books in this series, please contact our Customer Service Department at:

peterlang@presswarehouse.com (within the U.S.)
order@peterlang.com (outside the U.S.)

Or browse online by series at:

WWW.PETERLANG.COM

www.ingramcontent.com/pod-product-compliance
Lightning Source LLC
Chambersburg PA
CBHW050615280326
41932CB00016B/3060